Spiritual Gifts for Today?

HERBERT CARSON

KINGSWAY PUBLICATIONS

EASTBOURNE

ISBN 0 86065 456 7

Unless otherwise indicated, biblical quotations are from
the Holy Bible: New International Version, copyright ©
International Bible Society 1973, 1978, 1984.

AV = Authorized Version
Crown copyright

RSV = Revised Standard Version
copyrighted 1946, 1952, ©1971, 1973 by the
Division of Christian Education of the National
Council of the Churches of Christ in the USA

Front cover photo: Tony Stone Photolibrary—London

Printed in Great Britain for
KINGSWAY PUBLICATIONS LTD
Lottbridge Drove, Eastbourne, E. Sussex BN23 6NT by
Richard Clay Ltd., Bungay, Suffolk.
Typeset by CST, Eastbourne, East Sussex.

Contents

1

Split Churches

If evidence were required to demonstrate the continuance of sin in the life of the Christian, one need only note the sad way in which godly and Bible-loving believers can yet part company over some area of God's truth. It is not the revealed truths of Scripture that are to blame but our own sinful tendency to elevate our particular interpretation of a disputed passage to the level where it is the only acceptable Christian viewpoint. When we are dealing with what one might term the 'core' doctrines of the faith, the Scriptures are so plain that it is not surprising that down the centuries there has been a general consensus; witness the historic creeds and confessions of the churches. There are, however, areas of Scripture where the Spirit has not given us that same measure of plainness, and where Christians should match the Spirit's restraint with an appropriate reserve. Unhappily, we are too often prone to take passages concerning which equally godly and devout commentators have reached differing conclusions, and to see our own interpretation as being the only acceptable one.

Take, for example, the matter of the two great gospel ordinances, baptism and communion. Here, surely, we should find unity. Instead there has been not simply healthy debate, which would be desirable, but acrimonious controversy and bitter division. The leaders of the Protestant Reformation in the sixteenth century were divided on both sacraments. Luther, Calvin and Zwingli were deeply disagreed over the significance of the Lord's Supper which is, ironically, the sacrament of Christian unity. Even more tragically, all three were bitterly opposed to those whom they nicknamed Anabaptists or re-baptizers, and were ready to tolerate or even encourage persecution, in spite of the fact that a godly Anabaptist leader like Menno Simons stood with them on the great basic affirmations of the gospel.

One sees another tragic illustration of this sinful tendency to divide bitterly over biblical truth—in this case among the leaders of the Evangelical Revival that swept Britain in the eighteenth century and transformed the spiritual and moral life of the nation. On preaching Christ crucified, the need of the new birth and the call to holiness, there was unity of evangelistic purpose. Yet in the question of how the grace of God is mediated to the sinner there was deep and bitter division. To vast numbers of Christians the hymns of Toplady have been superb expressions of the deepest aspirations of the soul. It comes as a shock to discover how bitter in the doctrinal conflict the author of 'Rock of Ages' could be. To read the title of his sermon against John Wesley, 'An Old Fox Tarred and Feathered', is to be astounded at such vehemence. To read of Toplady rising from his deathbed to denounce Wesley is to be further shocked. That shock may well be compounded when we hear the great hymn writer Charles Wesley descend to the same inglorious level by scornfully dismissing his Calvinistic opponents. One can only marvel at the forbearance of God, and at the grace by which, in spite of their shared sinfulness, he yet used them both in such marked ways.

8

Why do Christians react to one another in such inconsistent ways? Why indeed do we sometimes misuse the word of God to buttress our own prejudices, traditions or novelties? One major reason—perhaps *the* major reason —is the sin that lay at the root of man's first disobedience in the Garden of Eden. It was pride that led first Eve and then Adam to ignore God's commands. Pride is self-interest, self-love, self-esteem. Pride wants pre-eminence and reacts with vigour, with passion and even with fury when our ideas are challenged, our plans thwarted or our comfort disturbed. Pride makes us so blind to God's gracious dealing that in our sinfulness we claim credit for the natural gifts of body or mind with which our Creator has endowed us. It is God who gives physical beauty or an attractive disposition, or skills, whether of hand or brain. Sinful pride, however, prompts us to preen ourselves on our own abilities and attainments.

To be born again is to become a new person with a new understanding. It is to be turned from being self-centred to being God-centred. It is rather like the revolution in astronomy in the fifteenth century when Copernicus asserted, in the face of much opposition, that it was not the earth that was the centre of the solar system but the sun. Modern astronomers accept this thesis as basic knowledge, but in Copernicus' day it marked a radical reversal of thought. There is a spiritual 'Copernican revolution' when the self-centred sinner becomes, by God's grace, the God-centred believer.

Sin, however, is persistent. All too easily we revert to what is now an abnormal attitude, with pride again in the ascendant. The graces and gifts of the Christian life, and the evangelistic endeavours and ministry to which these lead, are alike God's gracious endowments. Yet in our sinful folly we become proud of our orthodoxy, our spirituality or our zeal. We forget that if we have come to a clear grasp of Christian doctrine, it is because 'God, who said "Let light shine out of darkness," made his light shine in our hearts to give us the light of the knowledge of the glory of God in the face of Christ' (2 Cor 4:6). Likewise, if we adopt a superior attitude to others because we have received a spiritual gift, it is because our indwelling sinfulness blinds our minds to the obvious fact that the word 'gift' means neither reward, nor payment for services rendered, nor recognition of our essential worth. It means precisely what it implies in any other context, a freely granted token of someone else's favour.

If we have a firm adherence to the historic faith—one of the goals of an heir of the Reformation—we must keep reminding ourselves that it is only the mercy of God that has kept us from heresy. Similarly, if we have experienced the powerful working of the Holy Spirit either in our own life or in the life of our local church, we do well to recall that the very word 'charisma' roots every gift in the amazing grace of God. A smug orthodoxy and a superior air over spiritual gifts are alike not only self-contradictory but positively sinful.

Apart from the basic issue of human pride, there are other factors that have either produced sad divisions within the church or have exacerbated tensions already existing. There is, of course, the recurring problem of personality clashes. When strong-minded people see things very differently they are often on a collision course that will only be avoided by a mutual realization that they are both sinners. This realization should remind them both that they have much sinful failure in their own life and service, failure that should humble them into a greater tolerance towards fellow believers. Personality clashes, however, are not simply the product of the present debate. They have been an endemic malady in the churches down the centuries.

A further reason for bitter division is the failure to draw a clear distinction between the false teacher who is subverting the gospel, and the true believer who, because of his inadequate theology, his inconsistent living, or even his zeal without knowledge or wisdom, weakens the very witness that he is so anxious to give. That distinction between the enemy of the gospel and the inconsistent but true Christian is well set out in the first two chapters of Paul's letter to the Galatians. He recognizes in the fierce denunciation of chapter one that the false teachers are removing the very foundations of the gospel—hence his vehement and repeated 'anathema'. But when he turns to Peter, he still recognizes him as a brother even while being forced to resist his stance.

Paul neither makes the mistake of ignoring Peter's failure nor goes to the other extreme by denouncing him as if he were an enemy of the gospel. There is no hint of that flabby charity that hesitates to challenge, or an unbalanced passion that magnifies another's failure so as to present it as a serious crime against the gospel. If only inconsistencies and woolly-minded confused thinking were met with a Pauline loving challenge rather than a scornful dismissal, we might have been spared many of the divisions of the past and the present.

Allied to this failure to recognize those who are truly our brothers and sisters in Christ is the delight many seem to have in labels. Such can be either a shorthand form of abuse of an opponent, or a proudly worn badge of an adherent to one particular persuasion. Take the two terms 'Calvinistic' and 'charismatic'. The former has often been used contemptuously. With the prefix 'hyper' added it has been applied to those who, it is claimed, are not interested in evangelism, when in fact the truth is that they are not prepared to accept the particular techniques or methods of their accusers, or the theology that lies behind these methods. Similarly, a man in the ministry is quickly dispatched in some circles with the patronizing or even dismissive comment that 'he has gone charismatic', when what has really happened is that he has perhaps tried in all honesty to come to terms with areas of Scripture that formerly he neglected.

Like some of the famous nicknames fastened on believers by the world—the term 'Christian' is the most notable of these—the label often becomes a cherished badge. There are dangers in this. In the first place it can distort the witness in that it concentrates on one area of biblical truth to the neglect of others. Then again it can become an exclusive label, the mark of a club member who prides himself on membership and is quick either to deny its wearing to another or to expel from the club those who no longer meet the narrowly-defined criteria. Such label wearing or label brandishing, whether as a badge of identity or a term of abuse, are all too often the indication of a failure to attempt to understand why a fellow Christian sees some issue differently from ourselves. It can also be a defence mechanism to avoid the challenge of Bible truths that we have not really faced.

This defensive reaction points to a further factor in the divisions within the gospel community: namely, the fear, and the corresponding feeling of insecurity, both of which can be so inhibiting. It can be seen in the responses of men in the ministry—and I speak as one whose life has been as a minister of local churches! Because God may have opened the eyes of some in the congregation to see truths in Scripture that the preacher has not really considered, he may feel threatened. In the same way, if some members of his flock display a new evidence of spiritual life and power, especially if the prompting that led them in that direction came from a source other than his own preaching, he may feel his own position being queried. If those same members of the congregation display immaturity or lack of grace in their reaction to the regular life and ministry of their church, he may feel even more acutely what he sees as a challenge to his authority.

He may react by asserting all the more insistently his authority as minister. He may try to suppress those whom he sees as threats to the stability of the church, whether they are reformed zealots accusing him of Arminianism, or charismatic zealots charging him with deadness. In either case, he may himself precipitate a crisis that he will attribute to his concern for maintaining a biblical view of ministerial authority when, in fact, he is simply displaying the normal reactions of an insecure or frightened man.

This is not to say that there is not such a thing as the authority of the preacher. Ephesians chapter 4 makes it very clear that the ministry gifts are from the ascended Lord. However, that does not mean that the minister is the sole repository of biblical truth. Nor does it mean that the stage he has reached in his understanding of Scripture is the final one.

Spurgeon in his autobiography recalled the debt he owed to the theological acuteness of his grandfather's cook in Newmarket. His grandfather was a much-respected minister while the cook had no formal theological training and clearly never saw herself as either a theologian or a preacher. However, it was from the cook that he learned the basic principles which gave a doctrinal direction to his subsequent ministry. This willing acknowledgement of his indebtedness did not imply any reflection on his grandfather's ministry and certainly did not remotely hint at contempt. It was simply that he recognized that while God has graciously entrusted to those whom he calls to preach the word an authority to back their preaching, he never guarantees that they may not misuse that authority. Nor does he give his preaching servant such an exclusive insight into biblical truth that no one else in the congregation may be expected or permitted to contribute to what God has made known to them in the Scriptures.

Peter warns elders, identifying himself with them as a fellow-elder and, therefore, presumably liable to the same danger: 'Be shepherds of God's flock . . . not lording it over those entrusted to you' (1 Pet 5:2–3). A preacher's authority is made known not by his protestation, and certainly not by his complaints, but by the evidence of the anointing of the Spirit upon his ministry. In this whole matter of division within churches it is a salutary, and indeed sobering, reflection that while such divisions have often been caused by the impetuous and elitist behaviour of those who feel they have arrived at a superior position, it is also sometimes true that the cause of division lies in the stubborn intransigence of the leadership.

There is an irony in this matter. It is that those who would most heartily reject the Roman Catholic view of tradition, and also the Roman claims to new revelations, can themselves end up in a position not far from Rome. In the pyramid of the RC view of revelation, Scripture and church tradition are the twin sources of revelation, with the teaching office of the papacy controlling both. In popular terms, the church gives you the Bible, tells you what are the valid traditions, and then quotes the authoritative figure. We who are heirs of the reformers' protest recall their emphasis on *sola scriptura*, Scripture alone. Yet how often has a particular traditional interpretation become so inflexibly held that to deny it, or even to modify it, is seen as virtually an attack on Scripture?

Witness also the key role blazed for some by an acknowledged authority figure. There are discussions and magazine articles as to whether he took this role or that. As the authority figure has been removed by death to share in the fully revealed truth of heaven, he is no longer free to be questioned. So his real or possibly only alleged views are canvassed. It is as if to discover them would be to discover the final truth. All this forgets that while God has given many giants to his church over the centuries, they must never be allowed to usurp the prerogatives of the Lord of Scripture, who is both the author and explainer of Scripture, the Holy Spirit himself.

What is so sad in the present situation of conflict is that both sides of the debate too often fail to see that they in reality need each other. Using the terms 'reformed' and 'charismatic' neither as triumphant badges nor as derogatory epithets, but simply as a conveniently summarized description of two theological positions, the conviction lying behind this present book is that the two emphases are not opposed but complementary.

Those who are happy to be known as reformed thank God for the rich legacy of serious doctrinal study bequeathed to them by the leaders of that remarkable work of God, the Protestant Reformation. Furthermore, they gladly pay tribute to the debt they owe to the successors of the reformers, the Puritans of the seventeenth century. Simply because of the stature of the man, they recognize the pre-eminence of John Calvin, and are not surprised that men described their theology as Calvinistic, such was the stamp of his God-given genius. The great reformer of Geneva would probably have repudiated such a title, and we would sympathize since what, for convenience sake, we call Calvinism is simply the faith of the Bible.

In this past generation there have been two notable surges of blessing. About thirty to forty years back there was an increasing interest in a rediscovery of the forgotten treasures of Reformation and Puritan theology. That interest developed into a world-wide influence that transformed the preaching of innumerable pulpits, with a corresponding impact on congregations. In the past twenty years a further tide began to rise. Again it began in a small way as Christians began to speak with increasing enthusiasm about the work of the Holy Spirit in their lives. It spread until, quite spontaneously it would seem, it has erupted on a world scale.

Was one or other of these developments an aberration, as some would claim? I believe that in fact they were both evidences of God's gracious activity, and the tragedy has been that they have been seen to be in opposition. That both sides need each other is reflected in the weaknesses that have appeared when the truths to which the other group witnesses are neglected. The very grandeur of the reformed presentation of God's truth can therefore become, if we are not constantly alert to the danger, a merely intellectual affair. We may be impeccably orthodox and yet lacking in life and spiritual zeal. Christ can become a concept in our minds rather than what he should be, the master passion of our hearts.

On the other side of the theological fence, that is, when Christians have been foolish enough to erect a fence, there is also danger. In this case it is the danger of a spirituality that is not firmly rooted in Scripture, and as a result can be side-tracked. Narcissus was the youth in classical legend who fell in love with his own reflection in the pool of water. The term narcissistic has been coined to describe that obsession with oneself, which is so disastrous. This is the especial peril of the 'charismatic', who can end up in an unending quest for new and exciting experiences; this can drive good men in leadership to the foolish path of trying to satisfy this feverish concern by whatever means.

I recall the visit that Philip Hughes, the very able reformed theologican, paid to California in the early days of what later came to be called the charismatic movement. What was particularly interesting was that the invitation came from Anglo-Catholic circles whose new spiritual experience had led them to the Scriptures and so to a questioning of some Anglo-Catholic tenets. Because Dr Hughes, the editor of the theological journal *The Churchman*, was an eminent critic of Anglo-Catholicism, he was invited to visit them. Anyone who knew him would know that with his philosophical background he was the last man to be swept off his feet by a surge of emotion. It was all the more significant that when he returned to England he declared that he was persuaded that what was happening was a movement of the Holy Spirit.

However, and this is possibly even more germane to our present discussion, he paid a return visit from which he returned with marked concern. He was troubled, he said, because what had begun, in his considered assessment, as a movement of the Holy Spirit, was in danger of being institutionalized as a Movement—the capital 'M' was deliberate! While there was no questioning the reality of the spiritual experiences of those in whose lives God had worked, there was increasing concern that the possible slide by some into a morass of subjectivism was not being checked by a rigorous scrutiny of all teaching and every new practice in the piercing light of biblical doctrine.

The dangers of both sides have been deepened by a further factor, namely, the arrival of a new generation who have presented to them either a complete system of theology or a complete spirituality. The young Calvinists of forty years back struggled towards the truth that was beckoning them on; their successors have the whole theological system packaged and ready for acceptance. So too, the charismatic field is now so extensive, so thickly populated and so accepted that there is a great danger of simply embracing what can, in some circles, seem like a Christian sub-culture.

The surest antidote to these dangers at either extreme is the fruitful interaction of a biblical emphasis on truth and an equally biblical stress on experience. Without the constant challenge of biblical doctrine there is danger of the charismatic field being taken over by impulses that are simply psychological or even demonic. On the other hand, if the right insistence on the primacy of the mind is not to end in a barren intellectualism and an arid liturgical pattern, there is need of the ever-freshening experience of the life-giving power of the Spirit. A sterile intellectualism can quench the Spirit's flame; an unbridled and credulous spirituality can fail to test all things and accept what seems to be real but proves to be spurious. The charismatic experience needs the bridle of reformed doctrine to curb its excess, and to guide it into profitable development. The reformed thinker needs the spur of a concern for a deepening heart knowledge of the Holy Spirit's operations. Certainly it is no easy matter to keep these two biblical emphases together, but who has ever suggested that Christian living was easy? There will be tension. Yet it is a tension that, if wisely handled, should be fruitful.

2

The Spirit of Truth

Truth lies at the heart of all our knowledge and all our relationships. If the first step in a developed argument is false, then no matter how logical every subsequent step may be, the conclusion will be wrong. If a witness does not tell 'the truth, the whole truth and nothing but the truth', then even if the judge is utterly impartial and the jury wholly fair, the verdict will still be distorted by the perjury of the witness. If a man's solemn vows at his marriage are a cover-up for an undisclosed earlier marriage, the resulting bigamy is not a true relationship, either in the sight of God or in the judgement of the law.

To speak the truth is to describe things as they truly are, not as we would like them to be. To make claims for ourselves or for others that are true is to assert something that will not be falsified by subsequent disclosure. Truth is reality as opposed to mere appearance. Truth stands in irreconcilable contrast to deceit, falsehood, fudging and lying. Truth shuns what is ambiguous and thus capable of divergent meanings. Truth exposes the spurious and extols the genuine. Truth is as remote from falsehood as light is from darkness.

It is not surprising, therefore, that truth was such a

prominent word in Jesus' presentation of himself and of his gospel. This is particularly obvious in John's testimony, both in his gospel and in his letters. He records the life, death and resurrection of Jesus. He selects the miraculous signs that he includes in his narrative. He comments further in his epistles on the significance of the life of Jesus. All this he does because he recognizes Jesus as the one who not only speaks the truth, but embodies it in his own person. So he recalls Jesus' absolute claim, 'I am the truth' (Jn 14:6), and in his first letter he roots what he has to say in the experience he himself had of this living truth: 'We proclaim to you what we have seen and heard, so that you also may have fellowship with us' (1 Jn 1:3).

Thus the God who has spoken through Moses and the prophets and has spoken finally in Christ is 'the only true God' (Jn 17:3). The Old Testament consistently bears witness to this truth. The law had insisted that the Lord alone is to be worshipped since he alone is truly God. The prophets with their blazing denunciations of idolatry reinforced the same truth. When Jesus so strongly emphasized truth, he was thus echoing and complementing the testimony of the Old Testament.

Since Jesus is the final disclosure to men of the true God, he is himself the truth, and the gospel that points men to Christ is thus also designated the truth (Jn 18:37). John is not the only New Testament writer who speaks thus of the gospel, although he is a major user of this terminology; it is also used by Paul (2 Thess 2:12; 2 Cor 13:8; Eph 1:13, etc.) by James (5:19) and by Peter (1 Pet 1:22; 2 Pet 2:2).

Jesus thus claims, in the face of Pilate's cynical question 'What is truth?', that he has come to bear witness to the truth (Jn 18:37). Indeed, he insists that the mark of genuine Christians is that 'they are of the truth' and so they give heed to him because they recognize that he is the authentic witness come from the Father's presence.

That he is the authentic witness is confirmed by the wealth of testimony cited to support his claim to be the truth, and to speak the truth. The Father who sent him bore witness to him, not only by the striking and recurring witness spoken from heaven, but also by the signs and wonders that the Father enabled him to perform. At his baptism (Mt 3:17; Mk 1:11; Lk 3:22), at his transfiguration (Mt 17:5; Mk 9:7; Lk 9:35) and in the face of Gentile enquiry there was an audible confirmation from heaven (Jn 12:28) that Jesus was indeed 'the beloved Son'. This spoken testimony by the Father was accompanied by authenticating signs, signs that reached their climax in his resurrection.

There are other testimonies to the truth as it is revealed in Jesus. There is the cumulative witness of the Old Testament. This is the significance of the constantly repeated refrain 'that it might be fulfilled which was spoken by the prophets'. This also is the reason for the inevitability of what was going to happen to Jesus, for the Scripture must be fulfilled—it cannot be broken (Jn 10:35). Indeed, that is the reason for Jesus' great indictment of the Jewish leaders, that they searched the Scriptures and yet failed to see that those very Scriptures bore witness to him (Jn 5:39–40).

Jesus' own words bear witness to him. Those who are spiritually awakened recognize that they are not delusions of grandeur but words of solemn truth. The words he spoke were rooted in his eternal union with the Father: 'Even if I testify on my own behalf, my testimony is valid, for I know where I came from and where I am going' (Jn 8:14).

Other witnesses agree. John the Baptist, the forerunner, not only points emphatically to 'the Lamb of God' but is equally emphatic that he is simply a voice to bear witness to the Christ. The works of Jesus carry on the same testimony, although admittedly he viewed them as being secondary to his own spoken witness (Jn 14:11). The disciples also were his witnesses. He had them with him not only to teach them, but that he might send them out to teach (Acts 1:8).

Much of this revelation of the truth belonged to the very brief period of Jesus' early life, and particularly to the shorter period of his earthly ministry. That short season of glorious revelation would end with his return to the Father's presence. His next great public disclosure would be at his second coming at the end of the age. Yet in all the intervening centuries, there would still be the need of witness. His apostles would finish their course, and then the eye witnesses would have gone. Thus, as his imminent departure approached, Jesus gave his promises concerning the coming of the Spirit who would maintain the witness to the truth until the end of history and the dawning of the eternal glory.

Jesus spoke in vivid terms of ensuring that the disciples would not be left to struggle on with only the memories of the past to keep them going. 'I will not leave you as orphans; I will come to you' (Jn 14:18). So the coming of the Spirit would mean the coming of Jesus. It would not be his coming in bodily form. That must await the final consummation of God's purposes at the end of the age. Nevertheless, it would be a real coming. It would not be some mystical feeling that would stir their hearts. It would be Jesus himself, coming through his Spirit to be with them always. It is not surprising, therefore, that Luke begins the book of Acts with a reference to all that Jesus began to do and teach, as he had recorded in his former book. The plain inference is that the second book records the *continuing* acts and words of Jesus as his Spirit abides with his church in accordance with his final promise to his disciples: 'I will be with you always' (Mt 28:20).

The Spirit is also declared by Jesus to be the gift of the Father in response to the prayer of the Son: 'I will ask the Father, and he will give you another Counsellor' (Jn 14:16). Since the Father and the Son are one in the unity of the Godhead, it is clear why Jesus speaks of the coming of the Spirit as a coming both of the Father and the Son: 'We will come to [you]' (Jn 14:23). One of the early creeds put it like this: 'He [the Holy Spirit] proceeds from the Father and the Son'. Thus, through the agency of the Holy Spirit, the transcendent God who is our Father in heaven draws near to us as a felt reality; and the Son who is exalted at the right hand of power dwells in our hearts.

Since the God who comes in grace to us is 'the one true God' and since Christ who is 'the truth' dwells in our hearts, it is understandable why Jesus emphasizes that the Holy Spirit is 'the Spirit of truth'. Only as such could he fulfil the ministry of revelation and strengthening that the Father and the Son have entrusted to him.

To be the Spirit of truth may be understood in two ways, both of which are mutually complementary. In the first place he is the true Spirit whose claim to be the Spirit of God, revealing the mind and will of God, is thoroughly grounded in truth. He is thus the genuine Spirit, in contrast to the false spirits who emanate from the supremely false spirit, the devil, whom Jesus well described as 'a liar and the father of lies' (Jn 8:44). In the story recorded in 1 Kings 22 we see the judgement of God upon the kings in that a lying spirit is let loose among the prophets. Their witness has all the outward marks of the true prophet. Even the symbolic action by Zedekiah is reminiscent of similar actions by Jeremiah and Ezekiel. Yet the spirit who spoke through them was not the true Spirit, but a lying spirit.

There are warnings in the New Testament of the same thing. Jesus warns of false Christs and false prophets who will deceive many. Paul warns the Ephesian elders that it will be from their own fellowship that men will arise speaking what is false. John speaks of the false testimony that comes from the spirit of antichrist. Indeed, in the very chapter on spiritual gifts (1 Cor 12) Paul begins by rejecting the lying spirit that prompts a man to say 'Jesus be cursed'. He points by contrast to the Spirit of God who, as truth, testifies that 'Jesus is Lord'.

The further implication of the title 'the Spirit of truth' is that what he makes known is the truth. The devil, by virtue of his totally corrupted nature, utters lies. The Spirit, by virtue of his holy nature, speaks only truth with no admixture of error or falsehood. Paul develops this basic concept further by drawing an analogy between human thought and speech and the same activities within the life of the Godhead: 'For who among men knows the thoughts of a man except the man's spirit within him? In the same way no-one knows the thoughts of God except the Spirit of God' (1 Cor 2:11). It is because of the perfect unity of the three divine persons that when the Spirit reveals the word of God, it is with the unsullied purity of absolute truth that the disclosure is made.

We can draw further implications from these two basic contentions—that the Spirit of truth is not only the authentic Spirit of God but that what he reveals is the truth. It can be concluded that he must be utterly consistent in his speaking. There is no possibility of contradiction. Men may be committed to truthful speech, yet, because of our finite condition, we make mistakes that we have to correct. We learn new lessons that compel us to modify past statements. Furthermore, because of our indwelling sinfulness we are prone to exaggeration, to telling part of the truth, to stating the truth in such a way that it presents us in the most favourable light. None of these can possibly apply to the Spirit of truth. He is not growing in his understanding. He does not discover new truths that force him to modify what he has already said. He has no need to try and dress up his witness by slight distortions or exaggeration. Such is his holiness, and such the intimacy of his fellowship with the Father and the Son, that he always speaks the true words of God.

There are two areas in which this consistency can be seen; first of all within the Scriptures, and then in the life of the Christian, whether as an individual or within the fellowship of the church. Taking first the area of Scripture, it is a basic Christian conviction—one might say a fundamental axiom or starting point—that there is a unity and so a consistency within the Bible. We reject the ancient heresy of Marcion that sets the Old Testament against the New Testament in such a stark way that two different deities emerge! Similarly, we refuse to endorse the old liberal approach with its simple religion of Jesus and the developed theology of Paul, or the ideas of the first three gospels over against the fourth. Rather, we see a consistency within the canon of Scripture. We gladly recognize that the Old Testament is the preparatory revelation, since that fact is spelled out clearly, not only in books like Romans, Galatians and Hebrews, but also within the prophetic books of the Old Testament itself. Thus, Jeremiah in his prediction of the new covenant, and Joel in his vision of the age of the Messiah, point to a fulfilment yet in the future for them. Within the developing pattern, however, there is a coherence, an absence of contradiction, a mutually consistent total revelation. It is because the Spirit of truth was the one who moved men to write the Scriptures that there is this unity (2 Tim 3:16; 2 Pet 1:21).

The practical implication of this conviction is that one of the basic principles for the interpretation of Scripture is that of comparing text with text, passage with passage. That is why we set such store by a consideration of the context in which any biblical statement is found. By context we mean not only the primary context of the actual passage, but the wider contexts—the book in which it is found, the testament in which the book is located, and finally the complete sweep of revelation. Behind all this process of study and interpretation is the fundamental conviction that the Bible is a coherent whole. Behind this, in turn, is the ultimate conviction that the Spirit of God is the Spirit of non-contradiction and of consistency—he is, in short, the Spirit of truth.

There would be widespread acceptance of this position among evangelical Christians. We must, however, go further and apply all this to the life of the church. The individual Christian will testify to being led by the Spirit of God, whether in what may seem to be a minor decision or in such major issues as a call to the ministry or to a missionary situation. Similarly, the preacher may plead for the anointing of the Spirit on the word while an individual believer may claim to bring a prophetic message to the congregation. In all these cases the claim is being made, either openly or implicitly, that behind the confidence and behind the utterance is the Spirit of God.

How then are we to test such a claim? Surely it is not because of the fervour, or even the godliness, of the one who makes it. Godly men and women can still make grevious blunders! The test that will be applied in this present book, as far as the author is able to do so, is that of consistency with the perfect revelation that the Spirit has given in the Scriptures. This means that whatever purports to be spoken or written under the compulsion of the Spirit must face the test of scriptural evaluation. If it is truly from the Holy Spirit it will agree with what the Scripture has already said. The corollary is also very clear. If what purports to be a word from the Lord clearly contradicts the plain testimony of Scripture, then no matter how godly the speaker may be, no matter how much blessing that church is enjoying, the word is not from the Spirit of truth. It is neither the assurance of the speaker, nor the exuberance of the mode of delivery, nor the acclaim of those who hear—it is, rather, the testimony of the Spirit of truth that is the final criterion. In short, it is Scripture that is our supreme authority.

To try and draw a distinction between word and Spirit or between orthodoxy and life is utterly wrong. This attempt sometimes appears in the acknowledgement that although what had been said in a church service lacked scriptural warrant there was, it is claimed, yet an answering response in many hearts and they were evidently blessed. In fact, what is really being wrongly asserted—and this needs to be spelled out clearly—is that the Holy Spirit may say one thing in Scripture and something totally different, and even contradictory, in some utterance for which his prompting is claimed. Fallible authors and preachers can be guilty of this kind of failure. They may write one thing in a book and then contradict it in their spoken word. They are, however, evidently fallible and sinful. The Holy Spirit is neither. His testimony in Scripture is explicit and authoritative. When he speaks today there must be agreement with his own revealed truth.

The Glory of Christ

When Jesus promised the disciples the coming of the Spirit of truth, he spoke also of the ministry that the Spirit would exercise. It would be primarily one of revelation: 'He will guide you into all truth' (Jn 16:13). He would come from the Father and the Son, his coming would be the consequence of the Saviour's prayer, and he would disclose all that was needed of saving truth in order that they in turn might share it with others.

This final and all-sufficient revelation would focus on one point—the glory of Christ (Jn 16:14). That, in turn, as Jesus himself disclosed in his high priestly prayer in John 17, would lead to the glorifying of the Father. A glorious Saviour recognized as such by his people would be seen as the love gift of the Father who had given him to the death of the cross, and had shown his acceptance of Christ's sacrifice by raising him from the dead and enthroning him at the right hand of power.

The word 'glory' appears frequently throughout the Bible. It speaks of a display or open manifestation of the essential being of God. We use it in a derived and lower sense when we speak of a glorious spring morning. By that we mean that the clouds have gone and the sunshine is bathing hills and fields in a dazzling splendour. In fact what we are seeing is the open display of the powerful heat and light emanating from the sun. In a far more wonderful way, indeed in a transcendent sense, the glory of God is the outward shining of his indescribable essence. His love, his power, his goodness, his holiness, his righteousness—and all the other words that spring to mind when we speak of God—all are displayed in his glory, and that glory is seen in Christ Jesus.

To glorify Christ is not to make him glorious, any more than the ministry of Christ makes his Father glorious. God has an essential glory that can neither be augmented nor diminished. The Father and the Son are eternally divine, with an everlasting bond of love within the divine life. They do not become divine, nor do they become more loving. Rather, it is that what they are is made known. The sun behind the clouds remains what it is; it is the parting of the clouds that displays that heavenly body to human beings. So God dwells eternally in light unapproachable. Yet in his revelation of himself, the clouds of human ignorance are pierced, and the glory of God shines through to awakened and enlightened sinners.

It is the ministry of the Spirit thus to enlighten dark

minds and so to enhance for us the essential glory of God. 'The god of this age has blinded the minds of unbelievers, so that they cannot see the light of the gospel of the glory of Christ, who is the image of God' but by the Spirit's ministry 'God, who said "Let light shine out of darkness," made his light shine in our hearts to give us the light of the knowledge of the glory of God in the face of Christ' (2 Cor 4:4, 6).

The glorifying of Christ would not be some new ministry quite distinct from the ministry of Jesus of Nazareth. There is no place in the New Testament for an alleged age of the Spirit to follow the age of the Son! Rather, his ministry would be continuous with, and indeed explanatory of, Jesus' own earthly ministry. Jesus had already spoken of this aspect of the Spirit's ministry, and he continues in the same vein: 'The Holy Spirit . . . will teach you all things and will remind you of everything I have said to you . . . He will bring glory to me by taking from what is mine and making it known to you' (Jn 14:25; 16:14).

This glorifying of Christ will not be like some lesson imparted by an external teaching agency: 'He lives with you and will be in you' (Jn 14:17). Thus his work of revelation and his work of enlightenment will go hand in hand. He is the artist who paints the picture, and who then enables the pupil to grasp the significance of the work of art. So the Spirit draws aside the curtain of human ignorance to display to chosen men the glory of Christ. His further aim is that they may record what he imparts to them so that others down the centuries may read, and by the illuminating work of the same Holy Spirit of truth, understand the revelation of the glory of Christ.

In glorifying Christ, the Spirit of truth demonstrates his own consistency by the unity of biblical testimony. Whether it is the dawning of the hope of the coming

Messiah in the promise in Eden, or the representation of his work in the ceremonial law of Leviticus, or the increasingly precise prophecies of Micah or Isaiah, the Spirit never contradicts himself. It is no wonder, therefore, that Jesus could give such a coherent presentation of biblical testimony on the road to Emmaus. 'Beginning with Moses and all the Prophets, he explained to them what was said in all the Scriptures concerning himself' (Lk 24:27).

That same consistency continues in the completed revelation in the New Testament to which Jesus referred. After all, the New Testament writings are simply the embodiment in permanent written form of the apostolic testimony to Christ. Whether it is Matthew tracing Jesus' life back to his virgin birth and to the prophecies of the Old Testament, or Mark with his sharp, almost staccato, account of the activities of Jesus, or John looking back to the eternal Word who was made flesh, it is a united testimony presented by the Spirit of truth through human agency. The same pattern continues with Paul, Peter, John, James and Jude as they draw out the implications of the death, resurrection and ascension of Jesus, and point forward to his final glory.

In all the variegated presentation there is a coherent and consistent pattern as men of God, moved by the Spirit, commit the revelation to writing and testify with one voice, 'Jesus is Lord'. It is this testimony that leads us straight to the protracted passages of 1 Corinthians 12–14 wherein the gifts of the Spirit are seen as the continuing means employed by the Spirit in the church to declare the glory of Christ. Because the ultimate purpose is the same, and because the one who moved Christians, individually and as bodies of believers, to bear witness to Christ is the Spirit of truth, our understanding of the gifts and our use of them within the church are alike to be governed by the final authority of Scripture.

If then we are to test every word whether spoken or written, it will lead to firm rejection of what is clearly contrary to the Spirit's basic aims and method. He aims to glorify Christ and he realizes that aim by maintaining among his people a consistent testimony. How, then, can the claim be made that the Spirit may prompt people to glorify Mary? Yet this is precisely the claim made in some Roman Catholic renewal circles.[1] To claim that at one and the same time the Spirit of truth accords a solitary glory to Christ while elevating one of our fellow sinners to a glorious role in which she becomes the object of prayer and praise is surely to implicate the Spirit of truth in gross contradiction. It is, in fact, to add to the basic idolatry the further grevious sin of attributing human error to the Spirit of truth. The Spirit simply will not endorse such error! Nor will he permit anyone to usurp the glory that, as he insists again and again, must be accorded to Christ alone.

There is no room for any alleged or imagined disparity between doctrine and life, between orthodox belief and Christian conduct, between theology and exuberant worship. It is the one Holy Spirit who bears witness. It is the Spirit of truth who never contradicts nor modifies what he has laid down. In short, to be subject in the exercise of spiritual gifts to the discipline of Scripture is not to be subjected to some legalistic restrictions. It is, quite simply, to be subject to the Spirit himself.

3

The Gifts—Continuing or Temporary?

The word 'charismatic' has fallen on bad times! It has become the stand-by word for TV commentators and journalists. It may be a politician, an industrialist or a football manager who is in view. They are presented as charismatic figures. They have charisma. Or so we are told. In fact, what they have is energy or drive or power of leadership or a veritable genius in the area of stimulating other people. All these natural gifts and abilities are, however, far removed from the charisma of the New Testament, which often goes totally unnoticed by the world and certainly would not merit a rating in the TV assessment of what media people choose to call personality.

If instead of using an anglicized form of the Greek word 'charisma' we translate it into the English word 'gift', we find the same misunderstanding. A gifted man or woman in the judgement of popular opinion is one whose marked abilities elevate them to a higher level of excellence. To be gifted is thus to be in a position of self-congratulation. Once again this is remote from the biblical view. The gifted one in the New Testament is a spiritual pauper who has been enriched by God, a helpless sinner who has been given an inner dynamic of soul, a useless rebel against his Creator who has been endowed with spiritual power that makes him a useful member of the church of God. In short, the gifted man of the world reckons that the community is in his debt in view of that which he is able to contribute to others, while the Christian who is gifted sees the debt as being his—he is in debt to God who has given him abilities to serve his God and his fellows. His indebtedness should keep him humble.

It is, however, not only in the world but sadly in the church that the word 'charismatic' is seriously misunderstood. On the one side it is like a red rag to a theological bull. The instinct seems to be to react, sometimes irrationally, often ungraciously, and certainly often in an unbiblical way. Yet it is not only among those who suspect the word because of all that is associated with it in their minds that the word is misunderstood. It is also sadly misused by some who are happy to use it as a description of their worship, their church structures or their own personal stance. In their case it is human pride that corrupts what is good. It is sometimes also excitement in face of the unusual that leads them to excess or to self-advertisement. Paul faced this in Corinth where there was elitism and, as a result, sorry division in the church. He had no mercy on this spiritual one-upmanship. How can anyone pride himself for possessing what he neither purchased nor merited? How dare he presume to despise or denigrate a brother or sister in Christ because their gifts do not, in his judgement, match his? What such an elitist needs to learn is that a gift is, by definition, something freely given. The further lesson is that no gift is for personal aggrandizement, but for building up fellow believers.

In view of this welter of confusion and indignation surrounding the use of the word 'charismatic' it might be helpful to state what should be glaringly obvious, that the word is not some recently coined one; it emerges straight from the actual language of the Bible. If we accept that the authors of the books of the Bible were uniquely inspired by the Holy Spirit, then we must surely conclude that in whatever way the activity of the Holy Spirit and that of the human authors is related, it must have a bearing upon the actual terminology used. The Greek word 'charisma', and its plural 'charismata', are thus the end product of the work of the Holy Spirit. They are, in short, God's words. That consideration should be a caution to those who would use the term 'charismatic' as a theological term of abuse. It should also chasten those who have misused the word to enhance their own status or denigrate their ecclesiastical opponents.

At the root of the word is the Greek word *charis* which means grace. So the charisma is the gift of God's grace. This means that there is no price-tag attached, and no merit award designation. It is given without money, as Simon of Samaria had to learn (Acts 8:20). It is given not as an award for outstanding zeal or achievement, as the Corinthians thought, but as a completely undeserved benefaction from a generous and forgiving God.

One cannot, however, use the word 'grace' without being impelled to emphasize its essential nature by bracketing it with the epithet that, since the sixteenth century Protestant Reformation, has been its constant companion—sovereign grace. Behind each gift and behind the grace that bestows the gift, is the supreme factor of the sovereignty of God. He is influenced neither by bribes nor by human attainments. He acts neither because of present virtues, nor of potential achievements by the recipients of his grace. He is the sovereign God who chooses how and when and in whom he should act. Nor does he always explain why he acts. Nor should we have the temerity to try and put God in the dock to be subjected to our cross-questioning. He is Lord! He will act as he chooses. He is gracious and it is in grace that he enriches our impoverished lives in such a way that grace overflows to enrich others.

If we recognize that the gifts of God are the expression of sovereign grace, then we may be delivered from some of the false distinctions that are often drawn. There is, for example, the dichotomy, or so it is alleged, between the desire for charismata and the prayer for revival. This distinction is sometimes evident in the dismissive reaction to any discussion of the charismata. What is really important is that we should be concerned for spiritual revival. This is the only ultimate answer to the needs of the hour.

Revival, however, is a sovereign work of God. There are times when he comes in exceptional power. The churches are swept by the power of the Spirit. There is a depth of life and joy and power hitherto unknown and indeed unimagined. The impact on the community is inevitable as great numbers are converted. But, we ask in reply, what of the years when we are between such periods of revival? The prophet reminds us that we are not to despise the day of small things (Zech 4:10). While we long for the greatest blessings God may be pleased to give, we yet must also give ourselves to present tasks and responsibilities.

We do not cease to preach because we await the days when God comes down as he did on Whitefield and Wesley. We do not cease to hold our conferences or reach out to the community with the gospel because we await the day when the heavens will be opened. The present situation demands that we should be faithful now. That means that we should be searching the Scriptures daily to hear what God has to say to us now. There is an old saying about the danger of making the good the enemy of the best. That danger is present when we are so taken up with our hope of an unusual visitation of the Spirit that we neglect what he has to say to us now about his way of working in our lives, and in the life of the church.

Another false distinction must be resisted. It is that between a concern for an experience of the Spirit in the exercise of his gifts, and the commitment to the preaching of the word. This again is reflected in some of the dismissive attitudes that, perhaps not so strangely, reflect the same kind of superiority complex that is ostensibly being resisted. So a concern with the gifts of the Spirit is countered by a ringing affirmation that what really counts is the faithful preaching of the word.

But who is to preach? Surely it must be those chosen by God and anointed with power by the Holy Spirit. What indeed are they to preach? Is it not the Scriptures, and will this not commit the preacher to explore in his pulpit ministry the whole of Scripture? He will be constrained to preach from 1 Corinthians 12 and 14, Ephesians 4, Romans 12, etc. However, preaching from these, and from many a passage in Acts or the Gospels, commits him to an underlying presupposition concerning the charismata. Is he preaching about gifts that belonged to the apostolic period of the first century or that still continue today? It is an issue he cannot and dare not avoid.

There is a further false distinction. It is that which is drawn between the gifts of the Spirit and the fruit of the Spirit. The distinction is a true one if it simply emphasizes that we are discussing different areas of the Spirit's activity. It is a totally false one if it implies that the fruit of the Spirit is so important that our concern should be there almost to the extent of ignoring the issue of the gifts. Both, in fact, are vital to the well-being of the Christian and of the church. The Spirit develops within our lives the fruit of the Spirit that he may lead us on in holiness and true godliness. At the same time he purposes to use us to minister to one another within the life of the church. To

36

enable us to do that, he graciously imparts gifts to us. The fruit of the Spirit and the gifts of the Spirit are neither competing nor mutually exclusive. They represent, rather, parallel activities of the Spirit of God.

There is one important distinction to be drawn and one to which we will return later in greater detail. It is between the necessity to cultivate every single element in the fruit of the Spirit, and the recognition that no Christian will have, nor should expect to have, all the gifts. Contrary to the often misquoted version of Galatians 5:22, Paul did not refer to 'the fruits' but to 'the fruit'. The striking use of the singular is a reminder that every element is essential. A raspberry, for example, has in each single berry a cluster of miniature berries that together constitute the fruit. If one of these tiny constituents is mildewed or damaged then the whole raspberry is impaired. So with the fruit of the Spirit, each particular grace must be developing if the full fruit of the Spirit is to be seen. By contrast, in all the rich diversity of the gifts of the Spirit and in their widespread distribution, no Christian should expect to have all of them.

What men have parted assunder—fruit and gifts—God has closely joined together. Thus, in his great presentation of the gifts of the Spirit in 1 Corinthians 12 and 14, Paul included at the very heart of the statement his lyrical passage on love. Without that love, every claim to gift is pointless. Without love, gifts will be misused and sometimes in ways deeply hurtful to others. Yet love, it should be recalled, is first in the constituent elements of the fruit of the Spirit.

Having said that, we must put it the other way round. The statement in 1 Corinthians 12 and 14 surrounds the statement in chapter 13. In other words, love must be seen in action in the church. If that is to happen we must each one discover our role and place in the church. To discover those and to fulfil them we require the gifts that the Spirit will give us. The familiar biblical analogy of marriage may be helpful here. A young husband may love his wife very deeply and pledge himself to her. His love, however, will require him to help her in the work of the home. A facility in minor house repair work or mending electrical fuses is not unrelated to his relationship. It is simply a basic skill that enables him to express his love. So it is that the gifts of the Spirit enable the believer to express his love for the Lord and for the Lord's people.

However, we must return to the basic issue that underlies all consideration of the gifts of the Spirit. Were they confined to the first century or may we expect to see them today? To put it in terms of actual biblical passages, do 1 Corinthians 12 and 14 describe the situation that prevailed prior to the completion of the New Testament, or do they apply to us directly today? To use the familiar distinction—are these chapters descriptive or prescriptive? Do they show us how God met with believers in the first century, or do they present a pattern for church life in the twentieth century?

Before coming to a more detailed examination of what the Bible actually says, it is perhaps important to clear up some misconceptions, and make some general observations. As far as the misconceptions are concerned, I must emphasize the fact that to claim that the gifts of the Spirit are to be expected today is not the same as saying that all the phenomena that are seen today are of necessity the charismata of the New Testament. This needs to be stressed in view of the kind of argument that is often mustered. Thus, the objector begins not with the actual texts of Scripture but with the present situation. It is not very difficult to find illustrations of phenomena that are claimed to be charismatic but are more likely to be psychologically-conditioned responses to particular kinds of stimulus. It is no more difficult to find examples of people claiming to be gifted by the Holy Spirit who have divided churches, or who have produced excessively emotional situations, or who have lapsed into immorality. But, on the other hand, it is surely quite wrong to point to such excesses as proof that all claims to the continuance of the gifts of the Spirit belong to the category of the spurious.

After all, Corinth was not lacking in excess of various kinds. There were Christians who seem to have been hooked on excitement, just as there are today. There were confusion and division in the church. There was drunkeness at the Lord's table, and a tolerated immorality of a particularly perverted character. There were, in short, all the ingredients that would today be grist for the mill of the critic of all charismatic claims. Could such a church be seen as the temple of the Holy Spirit? Could such pride and excess be anything more than damning evidence of the hollow nature of their claims? In fact Paul knows it all, recognizes its ugliness and denounces it. He issues stern words of warning and summons them to repentance. Yet he still rejoices in the evidence of the Spirit's working (1 Cor 1:4–7). He sees them as God's temple even as they deface that temple (1 Cor 3:16–17). He warns them against dispensing or silencing those who are exercising a spiritual gift (1 Cor 14:39). So we must refuse to be committed to the conclusion that because some, or even many, claims today are evidently spurious or misguided, therefore all such claims fall into the same category.

A further misconception needs to be clarified. To claim that the gifts of the Spirit were intended by God to continue in the church is not to claim that in every generation of Christian history evidence must be adduced to show the presence of a wide range of the charismata. For one thing, the basic truth of the sovereignty of the Holy Spirit is a reminder that he not only imparts the gifts to whom he wills, but also when he wills. Furthermore, we have to take into account the realities of human sinfulness which have led in the history of the church to periods of decline as well as to times of spiritual awakening. They have led also to times when essential gospel truths have been so relegated to the background as to have been virtually forgotten. The doctrine of justification by faith lies at the heart of the gospel. Yet so great was the decline in the Middle Ages that when Luther began to preach it in the sixteenth century it sounded like a dangerous novelty that was subversive of moral stability.

It is also important to remember how unreliable some of the sources of accepted views of church history really are. Leonard Verduin pointed out that the Anabaptists of the sixteenth century, like many of their non-conforming forebears in the Middle Ages, have not left accounts of themselves.[2] The records that recall them have been drawn from their bitterest critics and foes. The records of the Inquisition in Spain are hardly an impartial reflection of the views and practices of the victims. As so much of the life of evangelical believers during the late Middle Ages was hidden in the obscurity that was their only defence against a persecuting church, it would be very dangerous to draw unduly from that silence conclusions as to what their views were on the issue of the gifts.

Turning then to some general observations. Those who deny that the charismata were ever intended by God to continue beyond the period of the apostles must face the implications of their argument. The inevitable conclusion is not simply that some charismatic claims are to be rejected, but all such claims. This, therefore, means that some verdict must be passed on those believers who make such claims—and it is clear that many critics of charismatic teaching still gladly recognize that those whose teaching they reject are still brothers and sisters in Christ.

These acknowledged believers must, however, be seen to be totally unbiblical in their contention. This implies either that they are deluding themselves or that they have been conditioned by a current hysteria or, most seriously, that their practices are demonic. Some critics will not hesitate to follow these implications. But they would do well to pause and reflect on the solemnity of what they are saying. They are asserting that what some Christians claim to be the work of the Spirit is simply the product of a fevered imagination, an impressionable receptivity or Satanic delusion. A salutary reminder is in place here: it was this kind of charge that the Pharisees made against Jesus.

A crucial statement as we discuss this matter is Paul's exhortation to the Thessalonian believers: 'Do not put out the Spirit's fire; do not treat prophecies with contempt. Test everything' (1 Thess 5:19–21). Here is the cautionary word that addresses both extremes in the present debate. There are those who need to be warned of the danger of being deaf to the Spirit's testimony and blind to his working. At the other extreme, where wishful thinking and credulity reign supreme, there is a firm reminder that not every claim can be substantiated nor every practice validated. Everything must be tested, and the touchstone is the criterion of Scripture. We are back to our basic position that the Spirit who gives the charismata is the Spirit of truth, and that means the Spirit of Scripture. So our standard is neither our church tradition, nor our own cherished position, nor, on the other hand, the enthusiastic acclaim of those who are sure that they have something fresh from God. Our standard, as ever, is the Scriptures. We must test claim and counter-claim by the Spirit's own testimony in the Bible.

Let me begin then with noting some of the general implications of a refusal to accept that the gifts were intended by God to continue within the church. In the first place, it means that a very substantial slice of 1 Corinthians is only indirectly applicable to our present situation. If the gifts were only for the first century, then the chapters simply become a descriptive recollection of what has long since passed. The long and detailed argument in chapter 14 about the use of the gift of tongues will only have antiquarian interest if in fact that gift has long since vanished from the life of the church.

It will not do to counter this by pointing to large areas of the Old Testament that no longer apply in a direct way to us. This counter-argument would insist that just as we may learn much from the book of Leviticus while the ritual has been abrogated, so we may learn about decency and order in church life even though the gifts that prompted Paul to consider the subject have passed.

In reply one must point to the fact that the New Testament nowhere supports this appeal to an analogy drawn from the Old Testament. There is certainly very clear teaching that the law of the Old Testament has been fulfilled in Christ and that the ceremonial law has been abrogated. There is also precise and detailed teaching, especially in the letter to the Hebrews, as to how we apply our study of the levitical system to the gospel age. There are, however, no such clear statements as to how we should apply these areas of the New Testament, which are claimed to be like the ceremonial law, only temporary. The reason for this silence will, I trust, become quite clear in the emphasis that follows—such teaching was not necessary for the simple reason that these gifts were not intended to be temporary.

There is a further consideration—it is that Paul spent a great deal of space to deal with what is now claimed to have been a very temporary situation. The book of Leviticus was to govern the ritual of the people of God for many centuries, from the time of Moses until the times of the Messiah. If the gifts were a passing phenomenon, why then should Paul give detailed instructions for something that would last less than half a century? Lest someone objects to my emphasis on the amount of material in view, it could be a useful exercise to compare the length of this section of the Corinthian letter with some of the shorter letters in the New Testament. It is almost as long as some, and longer than others, so that it can scarcely be seen as a small parenthesis.

It should also be noted that the whole section comprising chapters 12, 13 and 14 belongs together. It can easily be seen that chapter 12 is part of the continuing argument and chapter 14 resumes the flow. The verdict on chapters 12 and 14 as to whether they are descriptive or prescriptive must also apply to chapter 13, remembering, of course, that when Paul wrote the letter, the artificial divisions of chapters and verses did not exist. If then he is simply describing a charismatic situation in the first century are we to conclude that the central part of the section (now known as chapter 13) is also descriptive? Do we not need to love as we are commanded since it is not a prescriptive word?

A further general observation on this section of 1 Corinthians is necessary. It is to notice the reaction of the apostle to the acknowledged excesses in the pattern of worship at Corinth. He does not over-react. He does not reject the good as well as the bad in some sweeping denunciation. Because there has been excess he does not impose a rigid structure. In spite of the lack of balance and the wild enthusiasm, he resists the temptation to encase them in some kind of liturgical strait-jacket. His is a balanced reaction. He wants them still to retain the liberty that is their spiritual birthright, and he also wishes them to continue to exercise the gifts of the Spirit. What he does is to warn against letting liberty degenerate into licence, and to guide their zeal into biblically controlled channels. That should still be our aim today!

One part of chapter 13 comes prominently into view in the present debate. It is Paul's reference to the disappearance of tongues and prophecies and knowledge. This will happen 'when perfection comes'. The crucial question then is, when is this time of perfection? To those who see it as referring to the second coming of Christ, the passage does not refer directly to the continuance at the present time of the charismata. However, to those who argue against the continuance of the gifts of the Spirit, this is an important and indeed a crucial passage. To them the time of perfection is the time of the completion of the New Testament Scriptures. As this, in fact, took place within the lifetime of the apostle John, the period for the continuance of the gifts is, in this view, a very restricted one.

To be fair, not everyone who argues against the continuance of the gifts would interpret the passage in this way. Those who follow in the footsteps of commentators in the reformed tradition would be hesitant to accept such an interpretation. They might well point to John Calvin, the prince of Reformation commentators, to Matthew Poole, the seventeenth century Puritan, to Charles Hodge, or to John Gill. None of these saw the reference to the completion of the canon of Scripture but rather to the second coming of Christ. Spurgeon, in a magnificent sermon on 1 Corinthians 13:12, took the same line. The sermon, which bears the significant title 'Now and Then', points from our present limited knowledge to the perfection of heavenly knowledge and joy.

Victor Budgen, who makes this passage crucial to his argument, has to make a frank acknowledgement that 'it must be admitted that few commentators of the past expounded "perfection" in 1 Corinthians 13 to mean Scripture'.[3] He claims that there were some, and appeals to Jamieson Fausset and Brown in the nineteenth century. The actual words in this commentary are, in fact, a

44

comment on his claim. Referring to the phrases in the Authorized Version, 'shall fail ... vanish away' the commentator wrote 'Translate: "shall be done away with" i.e. shall be dispensed with at the Lord's coming being superseded by their more perfect heavenly analogues.' Victor Bugden was so keen to use the commentary's subsequent rejection of the continuance of the gifts that he ignored the basic contention that accords with other reformed commentators, that perfection refers to the Lord's second coming and to heaven. The commentary, after claiming the cessation of the gifts, reverts in the same passage to its basic admission: 'In one sense faith and hope shall be done away with, faith being superseded by sight, and life by actual fruition (Rom 8:24; 2 Cor 5:7).' The fact that the commentator himself quotes these two references reinforces the fact that the real reference of 1 Corinthians 13:10 ff. is to being absent from the body and present with the Lord.

J. C. Ryle had a saying when discussing commentaries: 'I call no man master'. I agree. Calvin, Poole, Hodge, Gill, Spurgeon and others of a reformed persuasion may all be wrong, though many of us would be hesitant about dismissing such giants quite so easily. We would need very strong arguments to persuade us. The question is, are the arguments for the rejection of their interpretation compelling? It is my own conviction that they are not. Indeed, I would go further and suggest that were it not for the exigencies of the argument about the charismata, the interpretation would have had a much less favourable reception. Some would claim it as decisive in favour of their rejection of any claim to charismata today. I would be rather more inclined to view it as a piece of special pleading. Let us turn, therefore, to the detail of the passage.

On the opening statement in 1 Corinthians 13:8 there can be little or no disagreement. Paul is reinforcing the emphasis throughout the passage on the primacy of love which abides for ever, not only before and after the formation of the canon of Scripture, but also before and after death and so for ever in heaven. By contrast, he is stressing the temporary nature of the charismata which will be done away with when perfection comes. Leaving for the moment the key question as to when this will be, it will certainly be agreed that Paul is referring not to some temporary lapse of gifts but to their final termination. The word he uses both of prophecy and of knowledge, in spite of the variations in the English translation, is the Greek word *katargeo*. It means to bring completely to nought, to nullify altogether. So it is used in 1 Corinthians 15:24–26 of whatever will be rendered void and useless at the coming again of Christ. Thus, not only the evil powers of hell, but death itself will then be made inoperative for ever. Earlier in 1 Corinthians Paul had used the word of the ending of the supposedly important things of this world (1 Cor 1:28), the rulers of this present age (2:6), the stomach and the food that satisfies its hunger (6:13) and finally, as we have noted, all lesser authorities and death itself. Clearly then he is speaking about the final and irrevocable removal of prophecy, tongues and knowledge. The question therefore presses in upon us, when will this happen?

Paul gives us the answer by contrasting his present condition with what he hopes for. He follows this contrast by giving a summary in verse 12 of his hopes. In verse 9 he acknowledges that his present knowledge and his present exercise of the gift of prophecy are alike partial. He is not saying that his present knowledge and his present prophecy are imperfect in the sense of being erroneous. Rather, they are referred to in terms of being partial. He knows, and yet there is so much more to know. He prophesies truth, but there is much wider truth yet to be known.

The illustration he uses of the relationship of childhood to maturity is introduced to illustrate the point. Childhood is a time when there is true knowledge, true thought and true speech. Yet it is all a stage in growth and development. With the advent of maturity the horizons widen, the balance is corrected and the reasoning is much more logical. Paul still identifies himself, as he does throughout the passage, with his readers. It is not just they whose knowledge is imperfect and whose prophecy is partial. He also is in the same situation.

Now Paul is deeply aware of his own calling to be an agent of God's revelation. In the next chapter he reminds the prophets of Corinth that his apostolic authority is the standard by which their prophecies are to be judged (1 Cor 14:37). Yet Paul, the author of infallible Scripture, acknowledges that he is still in an imperfect state and will only know fully when perfection comes. Is he really saying that he will reach fulness of knowledge when he has written his other epistles, and when the New Testament authors have completed their work? I find that very hard to accept!

My difficulty in accepting this interpretation deepens as Paul continues. Mirrors in the first century were usually made from beaten metal. They gave a rather inadequate reflection, hence Paul's reference to his present knowledge. It is like looking in a mirror. So he only sees rather dimly what is reflected there, but in the future he shall see the Lord face to face. Are we really expected to believe that Paul is asserting that the Christ whom he sees by faith as he writes 1 Corinthians is a blurred reflection compared with what will be seen when the New Testament is complete? That notion would seem to denigrate the infallible authority of this very epistle. Surely Paul is drawing the contrast between his present knowledge of the Lord which, though utterly true, is still imperfect when contrasted with the perfected knowledge of heaven.

Then he claims: 'we [and that includes Paul!] shall see [Jesus] face to face' (1 Cor 13:12). That will indeed be the glory of heaven. Jesus referred to it in speaking of those who despised his 'little ones' who believed on him: 'Their angels in heaven always see the face of my Father in heaven' (Mt 18:10). Stephen just before his martyrdom was given a foretaste of that heavenly vision: 'Stephen . . . saw the glory of God, and Jesus standing at the right hand of God' (Acts 7:55). Paul in his vision recorded in 2 Corinthians 12 and John on Patmos also had glimpses of that glory. Here, however, Paul speaks of that continuing eternal experience of knowing God.

Those who propound this rather modern interpretation point to the passage to which Paul seems to refer in 1 Corinthians 13:12. In Deuteronomy 34:10 the special nature of God's dealing with Moses is recalled: 'No prophet has risen in Israel like Moses, whom the Lord knew face to face'. There, it is argued, the phrase 'face to face' refers to revelation rather than to heavenly glory. But surely that succeeds in proving too much! Were Isaiah and Jeremiah, therefore, on a lower level as regards revelation? Was Moses alone the recipient of Scripture? Indeed, since Paul acknowledges that he has not had this experience, is he also to be relegated to a lower level? This certainly is novel doctrine coming from those who wax eloquent in face of the contention that there are two levels of prophecy. In actual fact, Deuteronomy is simply referring to the quite unusual mode of revelation. Moses was given what none of the other Old Testament writers experienced, a brief glimpse—and it was a fleeting one—of God's glory (see Ex 33:11, 20–23; Num 12:6–8. Yet he and the other prophets were on the same level as being recipients of God's truth.

Furthermore, the appeal to this verse in Deuteronomy succeeds in scoring an 'own goal'! Moses, to whom God spoke face to face, stood at the very dawn of revelation. Beyond him stretched the centuries of Old Testament revelation. Yet we are asked to accept that when Paul speaks of seeing God face to face it is in terms of the completion of revelation. In the Old Testament the exponent of this theory finds 'face to face' the key phrase to describe the first stage of God's revelation, while at the same time using it to try and prove that Paul is using it to establish that it is the last stage of revelation being implied in the phrase.

It is noticeable in the Greek text that Paul changes his use of words in the last two verses. When he is developing the theme 'now and then' he uses the Greek words *arti* and *tote* which mean precisely 'now' and 'then'. In the last verse he uses only one side of the contrast, 'now', and it is a different word, or rather a different phrase; instead of the simple Greek word *nun* meaning 'now', he uses the phrase *nuni de*, which may be translated 'now then' or 'so now'.

This phrase is used only in the New Testament by Paul and in the letter to the Hebrews. Furthermore, Paul never uses *nuni* by itself—it is used in this way by Luke in Acts 22:1 and 24:13—but always in connection with the additional word *de*. I have worked my way through the twenty times where Paul uses the phrase and in every one the reference is to a present situation or activity in contrast with what is in the past. He never uses it to contrast with something in the future. The two references in Hebrews are the same; the contrast is with what 'has been', not with what 'will be'. That is why the phrase can be used to describe what we are doing or experiencing now in contrast with the past, but also to introduce the final stage of an argument that sums up what has been said and leads to the final statement.

Thus in 1 Corinthians 13:12 Paul is summarizing the whole chapter. In view of all that he has written about the futility of any exercise of a gift or any activity for God if love is not present; in view of his extolling the wonder of love; in view of the contrast between present experience and future perfection—in view of all these he sums up: very well then, now then, or so now, in our present life the three great graces are the abiding realities, but the greatest, because it undergirds the others and will persist beyond the others, is love.

I feel almost like apologizing to my readers at this point. Many may well be saying under their breath, 'why is he spending such effort in rejecting an interpretation that in any case seems so far-fetched?' I can sympathize and can only say that I have been forced to do so because of the way this passage has been used to argue for the cessation of the charismata. It is significant that Calvin and the other great reformed commentators did not even mention this interpretation. Normally when there were different views as to how a verse or passage should be interpreted they would have presented them and given their own preference. In this case this interpretation apparently did not even strike them. We might say that they were all blind to the truth. We might, on the other hand, argue that it has only been the desperate need to try and buttress an argument against the continuance of the charismata that has led to the current popularity in some circles of an interpretation that really is quite a novelty, and a rather fanciful novelty at that, in the history of expounding the Scriptures.

Now then, if I may use Paul's phrase, having had to digress somewhat to deal with the suggested interpretation of 1 Corinthians 13:8–13, I must return to the main theme—were the charismata intended for the first century only or were they to be the continuing gift of the Spirit to the church? For the answer to that question let the appeal be to Scripture. Has the Holy Spirit in the New Testament moved any of the writers to state, in the same clear way in which Hebrews declared the abrogration of the levitical ceremonial, that in fact the charismata belonged to that same category of temporary provisions? To say that the levitical ceremonial was passing is not to ignore it or despise it. Like the scaffolding of a growing building, it was essential for a time and, that time having passed, it has been firmly relegated by the New Testament to things now past. Nowhere, however, is there a similar clear and decisive statement that the charismata were like the scaffolding of the apostolic church designed, like scaffolding, to be of temporary use.

Certainly it is clear that the gifts are seen in their function as witnesses to authenticate the apostles' ministry A key statement here is Hebrews 2:3–4:

> This salvation, which was first announced by the Lord, was confirmed to us by those who heard him. God also testified to it by signs, wonders and various miracles, and gifts of the Holy Spirit distributed according to his will.

There is no obscurity here. The eye witnesses were those who had accompanied the Lord and witnessed his post-resurrection appearances—the two criteria used for electing Matthias to the place left vacant by Judas Iscariot. The miracles and various gifts were thus the Holy Spirit's authentication of the apostolic testimony.

This statement fits into the wider biblical context where miracles did not happen in some haphazard fashion but were granted at the high moments of divine revelation: in the Old Testament, at the coming of the Messiah and in the initial outpouring of the Holy Spirit. It also squares with John's employment of the word 'signs' to describe the miracles of Jesus. They were wonders in that they elicited astonishment and scrutiny. They were powerful works in that they displayed the power of God. They were 'signs' in that they pointed beyond themselves to the glory of the Christ who performed them.

One can therefore fully appreciate Paul's appeal to the miracles that God wrought through him as 'the signs of an apostle' (Rom 15:19; 2 Cor 12:12). His special appointment as an apostle on a level with the Twelve was open to attack by hostile critics. He pointed, therefore, to the attestation given him by the Lord.

The inference that has been drawn from these clear facts is that since the apostolic testimony has been authenticated, and since that same apostolic testimony has been permanently embodied in the written books of the New Testament, the authenticating signs, being no longer needed, have been withdrawn. The analogy of the levitical ritual could be cited again. The fact that Jesus had offered the one final sacrifice and had been vindicated by God's acceptance of that sacrifice through the resurrection and ascension, pointed to the abrogation of the old sacrifices and the old priesthood. But inference is not the only reason for claiming that they have been abrogated. There is clear explicit statement to emphasize this. There is, however, no such clear statement concerning the charismata. Nowhere is it declared that they have passed away. Indeed, in various parts of the New Testament there is the very opposite kind of statement. So, I maintain, inference is not enough. We need explicit statements or clearly delivered arguments. Such are not forthcoming.

On the other hand, there seem to me to be clear statement and also inferences that the New Testament writers themselves draw, rather than later commentators. Take as our starting point Luke's account in Acts 2 of the happenings at Pentecost. What is of special importance is the prophecy of Joel that Peter declared had been fulfilled. In face of the questioning crowd with their perplexity and the claim by some that the disciples were drunk, Peter points them to Joel's prophecy. What they were seeing could only be understood if they realized what the Holy Spirit had said through Joel. The Spirit's testimony in the Old Testament prophecy was essential to understand the Spirit's activity now that the dawn of the day of the new covenant had come.

Joel had pointed forward to an extraordinary out-pouring of God's Spirit. Was this to be for that generation only? Were later generations simply to consolidate the position established on the day of Pentecost? The very words that Joel used suggest that this interpretation is totally inadequate. He pointed not to one brief period at the beginning of the gospel age when signs and wonders would authenticate the message. He pointed, rather, to the whole sweep of the age of Messiah right up to the time of the second coming of the Messiah. The activity of the Holy Spirit and his bestowal of gifts would thus continue.

The first phrase that points to that conclusion is 'the last days'. That phrase is used in the New Testament to speak of the initial period of special revelation through Christ, witness the opening of the letter to the Hebrews: 'In these last days [God] has spoken to us by his Son' (Heb 1.2; see also 8:8, 10; 10:16). It is also used of the period of growing spiritual darkness prior to the glorious coming again of Christ (see 2 Tim 3:1; Jas 5:3; 2 Pet 3:3). It cannot therefore be limited to the first century. It embraces the whole period between the day of Pentecost and the second coming of Christ.

A further significant phrase from Joel is ('all flesh' 'all people' in the New International Version). It is used in various places in the Old Testament to speak of all nations, all mankind. So in the days of Noah 'all flesh' was under judgement (Gen 7–9). Isaiah looked forward to the world-wide diffusion of the good news that would lead to 'all flesh' coming to worship (Is 66:23). Jeremiah (32:27) and Zechariah (2:13) used the same phrase as they spoke of all mankind. Thus, the outpouring of the Spirit was to be for all the nations. It was not simply for the Jews of

Peter's day, nor for the natives of the Mediterranean world reached by Paul's ministry. It summoned 'all people everywhere to repent' (Acts 17:30). It promised the Spirit to 'all who are far off' (Acts 2:39). So the closing words of the quotation from Joel speak of 'everyone who calls on the name of the Lord' being saved (Acts 2:21).

If then the outpouring of the Spirit is for the whole age until 'the great and glorious day of the Lord', and if it is intended for the blessing of all the nations, then surely the signs and wonders must not be limited to one brief period. The charisma to which Joel especially pointed was prophecy. However we may interpret that, it is clear that it was intended to be exercised among the nations and during the whole period of gospel preaching. While there was a rich diversity of peoples present on the day of Pentecost, they were but a tiny sample of a vast number. It would be a long time before Mongolians or Eskimos or Aborigines would experience the blessings, but their time would come, as it would for 'all flesh'. To limit the bestowal of the charismata to one brief period is surely to fly in the face of Joel's prophecy.

In this regard, there is a striking item in the list of gifts in Romans 12:6–8. The distinction is usually drawn, by those who reject the continuance of some of the charismata, between those that were temporary and those that were intended to continue. Now in the list in Romans 12 they are, by and large, continuing gifts. Yet on the basis of this argument there is one exception, namely, prophecy. There is no hint, however, in Paul's words that it is exceptional. To any reader of Paul's letter the various gifts seem to belong together. Surely, had prophecy been such an unusual phenomenon attention would have been drawn to the fact.

This raises the further query that must be put to those who reject the continuance of the charismata. Who is to decide which gifts continue and which have ceased? When Errol Hulse wrote his book *The Believer's Experience* (Carey Publications) on the Spirit he had to admit that it was difficult to decide whether the gifts of wonders and knowledge belonged to the temporary or the permanent category. My personal comment to him at that time was that it showed how arbitrary this division really was! In fact the decision as to which is deemed temporary and which continuing does not emerge from the text of Scripture, but from the pre-suppositions of the reader. It is surely a far more satisfactory procedure, and one that does justice to the biblical evidence, to cease this arbitrary process of inclusion and exclusion, and to accept all the gifts of the Spirit as being his continuing gracious provision for his church.

Before turning to a more detailed survey of the charismata, which will also develop further the argument for their continuance, it may be useful to record at this stage the words of John Owen, the prince of seventeenth-century Puritan theologians. His words are all the more significant when set in the context of his rejection of so many claims as spurious and as a hindrance to gospel preaching. Furthermore, he did not accept the continuance of the offices either of apostle or evangelist. Yet still he wrote: 'There was no certain limited time for the cessation of these gifts . . . It is not unlikely, but God might, on some occasions, for a longer season put forth his power in some miraculous operations, and so he yet may do, and perhaps doth sometimes.'[4]

4

For the Common Good

We need to keep reminding ourselves that Paul was not writing a doctrinal essay on the charismata. It was in the context of a pastoral letter to a local church that he discussed not only the gifts of the Spirit but many other issues as well. In all that he wrote his concern was to see the churches to whom he ministered built up and strengthened to serve the Lord. Hence his firm emphasis that the gifts of the Spirit are given 'for the common good' (1 Cor 12:7).

Such is our innate pride and our continuing sinfulness that we even pervert God's gracious gifts to us. This was exactly what was happening in Corinth. The Holy Spirit had abounded in generosity to the believers there. They had been given a variety of gifts to be used for mutual benefit. Pride, however, led to self-congratulation. Selfishness produced an inward-looking excitement that ignored the needs of others. This is a continuing danger and the answer is still the same: every blessing God gives and every gift he bestows are 'for the common good'.

It is by the power of the Spirit that Christians come to birth spiritually. It is by the same Spirit that they are united together in the shared life of a congregation. A church is not the product of the decision of a number of people to come together for shared worship and witness. Clearly there is such a decision when a church comes into being. Yet behind the decision is the supernatural activity of the Holy Spirit. The church that thus comes into being is the dwelling place of the Spirit. It is, to use Paul's phrase, 'the temple of the Holy Spirit'. It is within this temple that sacrifices of praise and thanksgiving, the sacrifice of the bodies of the worshippers and the offering of their gifts are presented to God. All this activity is prompted and directed by the Spirit.

When the Spirit first works in a sinner he unites that one to Christ. That is why Paul can write to the Galatians: 'I have been crucified with Christ and I no longer live, but Christ lives in me' (Gal 2:20). That means that within a church believers are united in fellowship with each other because they have already been united with Christ. Hence it is that Paul uses the analogy of the human body with its various limbs. 'You,' he writes, 'are the body of Christ, and each one of you is a part of it.'

Thus the building up of the church is part of the basic ministry of the Holy Spirit, which is to glorify Jesus Christ. The healthy functioning of each part of the body of Christ is not only with a view to mutual support within the body, but is ultimately aimed at glorifying the head of the church himself.

The key factors in the outworking of all this are twofold: there is one Spirit and the body is a unity. Because there is one Spirit, he is sovereign over every member. He it is who decides what gifts to allocate and when to bestow them. Because he is one and because he promotes the unity of the body, he will not introduce discord within the body. Where such disharmony emerges it is not and cannot be because of the Spirit's activity. It is, as it was in Corinth, because Christians either misuse the gifts or lay claim to a gift when evidently it has not been given, or urge people to lay claim to gifts without reference to the sovereignty of the Holy Spirit.

In the normal healthy functioning of the human body the ultimate control point is in the brain. Someone on a life-support machine in an intensive care ward may give the appearance of being either asleep or unconscious. In fact, the brain may have died and it is only the machine that gives the illusion of continuing life in the rest of the body. When the machine is switched off it soon becomes tragically obvious even to the non-medic that the person has died. It is the healthily functioning brain that controls all the complex mechanisms of the body.

So it is with the body of Christ. He is the head and only when his control is fully acknowledged and obeyed will the church function as God intends it should. There can, of course, be activity within the church, but if it is not controlled by Christ it does not have the purposeful direction essential for healthy functioning. Again it is like the human body in which injury can lead to opposite extremes, both of which are only too obviously abnormal. There is at one extreme paralysis in varying degrees and at the other the frenzy of unco-ordinated bodily actions. Too often in church life similar conditions can be seen. There can be a virtual paralysis of effort with a church giving little evidence of life. There can, by contrast, be an enormous amount of effort. Sometimes the activity may be quite feverish. Yet it is sadly evident that it is a kind of spiritual frenzy. Only when Christ the head is in control will there be activity that will glorify God. It is the Holy Spirit who both prompts this activity and imparts gifts to each member to fulfil a mutually supportive ministry.

The incorporation of the believer into the body of Christ is described by reference to the baptism that each one receives, 'For we were all baptised by one Spirit into one body' (1 Cor 12:13). It is an appropriate word to use since baptism in water is the initiatory ordinance of the Christian life in contrast to the other ordinance, the Lord's Supper. Baptism stands at the threshold of Christian experience while communion is a continuing observance throughout. Thus Peter's word to those awakened by his preaching is 'Repent and be baptised, every one of you' (Acts 2:38). This is the regular pattern of the Acts. When men and women turn to the Saviour, they are baptized and added to the company of believers. It may be a traveller on a desert road with a pool by the roadside as the baptistery. It may be conversions at midnight when doubtless the ordinary bath in the house was used. Yet in every case baptism is closely linked with the initiation of the new believer. We have rather lost sight of this with the tendency to defer baptism until a later date. As a result it becomes the sign of developing maturity. It was not such a sign in the New Testament. Rather, it was the sign of the new birth. Its vivid symbolism of death, burial and resurrection emphasized this. No wonder, therefore, that it was the first step of obedient faith for the new convert.

Some readers may already be objecting! Am I not confusing water baptism and Spirit baptism? Are they not two different things? By way of reply, I would first of all note two significant points. In the first place the very use of the term 'baptized' is surely linking the spiritual experience with the well-known baptismal practice of the New Testament. Why indeed should Paul now, and Jesus earlier, use this word 'baptized' if it did not have its roots in the practice?

In the second place, a study of New Testament usage will show that the writers did not always make the sharpest of distinctions between the thing (baptism) and the thing signified (the new birth). The two were so closely related in their minds that they tended to use the ideas interchangeably. A notable example of this is Peter's statement: 'Baptism . . . now saves you'. Because some might pervert this to produce a mechanical or quasi-magical view of baptism, Peter immediately qualified his statement by adding, 'not the removal of dirt from the body but the pledge of a good conscience towards God' (1 Pet 3:21). In short, he can speak of the symbol as if it were the reality that it signifies, so close is the relationship.

All of this leads to two conclusions. First of all, when Paul spoke of being 'baptized in the Spirit' he was referring to our initiation into a new sphere—it is a commencement symbol. Secondly, behind the reference to being baptized in the Spirit is the whole symbolic usage of an ordinance in which death, burial and resurrection proclaim in vivid picture language that the believer has died to his former life and has been inaugurated into a new life.

To examine the phrase 'baptized in the Spirit' more closely one has to turn to the usage elsewhere in the New Testament of the self-same phrase—and it is most important to notice that it is exactly the same phrase, using the same preposition 'in' in every case. The first four occurrences refer to the same statement for they are the recall by all four evangelists of the words of John the Baptist: 'I baptise you in water for repentance. But after me will come one who is more powerful than I, whose sandals I am not fit to carry. He will baptise you in the Holy Spirit and with fire' (Mt 3:11mg; also Mk 1:8; Lk 3:16; Jn 1:33). The two occurrences of the phrase in the Acts are both references to the same statement, first of all by Jesus to his disciples (Acts 1:5) and then by Peter (Acts 11:16). So all six references really become one reference to the words of John the Baptist.

In John's words it is clearly Jesus who is the baptiser who stands in contrast with John; Jesus is the Messiah over against John the forerunner. In John's ministry the element in which he immersed people was water, whereas in Jesus' ministry it is the Holy Spirit. It is most important to emphasize that in every case it is the same Greek preposition (*en*) that is used. In the English translations this identical preposition has been translated in different ways; when applied to John's words by the preposition 'with' and in 1 Corinthians 12 by the English word 'by'. In the margin in each case the literal meaning is given and in all cases it is the identical preposition 'in'.

This is not a quibble about translation for it can lead to a fundamentally different interpretation of the phrase. So in using the word 'with' it clearly shows that as John baptized using water as the element, so Jesus baptized using the Spirit as the element. If, however, 1 Corinthians 12 is translated as 'by one Spirit', one can then draw the conclusion that it is not Jesus who is the baptiser but the Spirit.

Now some may argue that the Greek preposition may be used in varied ways and thus be validly translated either as 'in', 'with' or 'by'. This is a valid point but only if we are discussing the preposition in isolation. In the present case we are not dealing as a dictionary might with one word, but with a whole phrase. Indeed it is more than the phrase 'in the Spirit' that is repeated. In each case it is linked to the term 'baptized'. This surely leads to the most reasonable conclusion, namely, that the statement of John and the statement of Paul are parallel. To say that in one case Jesus baptizes and in the other that the Spirit baptizes is to give the same word two different meanings even though the terminology is identical. It is a much more natural use of words to see them as the same in their essential meaning.

To sum up this rather detailed argument, I am maintaining that Paul, in using the word 'baptized' is using a word that throughout the New Testament always refers to an initiatory experience, whether it is referring to an outward ordinance or to the more spiritual reality of which the outward ordinance is a vivid sign. Furthermore, in every case it is the Lord Jesus who initiates the believer by means of the baptism that he administers. John employed water to point sinners to the need of cleansing and thus he had repentance in view. With Jesus it is the Spirit in whom he immerses the believer. In this case it is not the believer's response that is in view as with John's repentance, but the Spirit's powerful purifying effect. So he 'baptizes in the Holy Spirit and in fire'. In the Greek the second 'in' is not there! This suggests that 'Spirit' and 'fire' are, as it were, tied in the same bundle. It is not as if there is some separate element. Rather, it is the Spirit in his purifying work who is the element in whom Jesus immerses us.

This in no way rejects the truth that God may meet with the believer in a special and even an overwhelming way subsequent to his conversion. Indeed, Paul not only prays for Christians that God may thus work by his Spirit to lead us to new depths of experience of the love of Christ (Eph 3:16), he also points to a spiritual fulness that is to be our constant goal: 'Be filled with the Spirit' (Eph 5:18). It is noticeable, however, that never in the New Testament is there prayer that believers should be baptized in the Spirit. Never is there a command for believers to be baptized in the Spirit. Never is there an urging to seek this baptism. There is, however, evidence both of prayer and command to be *filled* with the Spirit.

Some may point to the experience of the disciples on the day of Pentecost as a total repudiation of the arguments just used. Were the disciples not believers before Pentecost? Was Peter not already enlightened at Caesarea Philippi (Mt 16:17)? Did they not experience the Spirit in the upper room? (Jn 20:22). The answer to these questions is, of course, 'Yes!' At the same time it must be emphasized that Pentecost, like Calvary and the resurrection, was a unique historical occasion. It was the beginning of the new age. It was the inauguration of the new covenant to which Jeremiah had pointed centuries before. The disciples had the unrepeatable experience of belonging to both sides of the history of revelation. They were Old Testament men who became New Testament men. They belonged to the generations who had awaited with eager anticipation the coming, the death and the resurrection of Jesus. They also belonged to the generations among whom we are numbered who look back to these great foundation events. It is in their location, at the watershed of the history of redemption, that makes them unique. In that sense they never could be typical. John Stott put it very well when he pointed to the very different descriptions in Acts 2 of the two groups of believers:

> This distinction between the two companies, the 120 and the 3,000, is of great importance, because the norm for today must surely be the second group, the 3,000, and not as is often supposed the first. The fact that the experience of the 120 was in two distinct stages was due simply to historical circumstances. They could not have received the Pentecostal gift before Pentecost . . . We live after the event of Pentecost, like the 3,000. With us, therefore, as with them, the forgiveness of sins and the 'gift' or 'baptism' of the Spirit are received together.[5]

Writing from a very different theological perspective from that of John Stott, David Watson recalled in his autobiography the time when God met him in a new and powerful way. I can recall that time well as David was a near neighbour of mine in Cambridge and it was abundantly evident that, evangelical though he had been, and gospel preacher that he had been, he had had a fresh and overwhelming experience of the Holy Spirit.

He recalled rushing round to his friend Basil Atkinson, a father-figure to many in Cambridge at that time. His exuberant testimony showed his delight: 'I've been filled with the Holy Spirit.' Subsequently he visited Dr Lloyd-Jones in Westminster. The latter listened and then said 'You've been baptized with the Holy Spirit.' Those who have read Dr Lloyd-Jones' sermons on Ephesians 1 published by the Banner of Truth will know that he viewed baptism in the Spirit not as an initiatory experience but as a later blessing that the Christians received by an act of God, as sovereign in its grace as when God visits the church in revival; I have heard Dr Lloyd-Jones use that very analogy.

David Watson, on his return, considered what he had heard and how his experience had been described. However, he wrote on reflection that he felt, with great respect, that Dr Lloyd-Jones was mistaken. It was not that he questioned the reality of the experience. There was no gainsaying that powerful coming of the Spirit to his soul. It was simply that he believed that his spontaneous outburst to Basil Atkinson was in fact the biblical terminology. He and Dr Lloyd-Jones were describing the same gracious work of divine grace. David, however, believed that the biblical description was not 'baptism in the Spirit' —that refers to the initiatory work whereby Christ baptizes us in the Spirit into his body. The biblical terminology, David maintained, was 'filled with the Spirit'.[6]

He might well have pointed to the great prayer meeting recalled in Acts 4:23–31. Here were men and women who had gone through the mighty experience of the day of Pentecost. Here again, however, there was something new that yet echoed Pentecost: 'The place where they were meeting was shaken. And they were all filled with the Holy Spirit' (Acts 4:31).

We return again to the theme that introduced this chapter. We have been baptized into the body of Christ. By the powerful working of the Spirit we have been united not only to the head of the church but to our fellow members. Our growth in grace and in holiness emerges from the continuance of that living union as, through the Spirit, Christ lives in our bodies to make them his dwelling place. At the same time our growth in usefulness to each other emerges from the bestowal by the Lord of the gifts that are given to us 'for the common good'.

Because gifts are given to us for the common good, there is no room in the church for party spirit nor for factions or cliques. Nor is there any place for the divisions that characterize the world. There can be no room in the church for racism or snobbery of any kind whether social, economic or educational. We are all debtors to mercy. We are all committed to minister to others as the Lord has ministered and continues to minister to us.

Because no one believer has all the gifts, each one of us is dependent on others. The New Testament picture of the church is not one of a collection of individualists attempting to maintain a sturdy independence of all the others. There is, rather, an interdependence between one Christian and his fellow believers. The church is not a religious organization developed by human initiative. It is a living organism in which, as in every living body, every limb must fulfil its function if it is to contribute to the healthy functioning of the whole.

The living body has its beginning in the moment of conception as life is imparted. There is a vast gulf between the most beautiful and complex doll and the most ordinary baby. It is the difference between an organization of the elements of a toy into a unified piece of craftsmanship, and an organic union of living parts in a vibrant unity. The living body, from that moment of conception, develops as the bodily cells divide and multiply. So the church is an organic whole with multiplying cells in the activity of witness so that growth continues.

In a healthy body all parts are there—there is serious impairment if a limb is amputated. All limbs must also be alive and if gangrene sets in a limb ceases to function, and indeed its deadness will spread to destroy other limbs. In the third place, all these living limbs in their totality must be functioning in harmony under the direction of the brain. So Paul works out the analogy in the life of the church. The Spirit who imparted life at the beginning continues to sustain life. It is through these living limbs in the body of Christ—these Christians in whom the Spirit dwells—that the church is built up.

The harmony of the body means not only, as we have seen, that there must be no proud spirit of independence. While there must be no self-sufficiencey, neither must there be an attempt to dominate others. Each of us is there for the good of others. Because we belong to Christ we also belong to each other. In serving one another we are serving the Lord of the church himself.

This means that there are no unimportant members in the body of Christ. While some may play a more obviously public role than others, all of us have significance. All of us have a distinctive contribution to make. While we must avoid the pride that wants to excel for self-gratification, we must also avoid the false modesty and the self-depreciation that are alike a denial of what God has done for us.

Paul uses the language of absurdity to emphasize the point. One limb cannot opt out of its union: 'If the foot should say, "Because I am not a hand, I do not belong to the body," it would not for that reason cease to be part of the body' (1 Cor 12:15). You cannot have a body that is all an eye or an ear. So he stresses that it is equally absurd for any one believer to try and play every role in the life of the church as if he or she were the only member in the church.

There is, in fact, no limb or part of the body that is without value. We notice that when we stub our little toe on the bed: it will obviously impair our walking. A man with a small cut in his thumb will find it very difficult to button the top button on his shirt! We discover that the scarcely-noticed parts of our body are enormously important at certain points. So it is with the body of Christ. The leaders and the led, the preachers and the hearers, the authors and the readers, the helpers and the helped—all have their place and all require their own individual equipment for the particular ministry that they exercise. It is the Spirit's work to equip each member with the gifts that will enable that member to make his or her own distinctive contribution.

People have spoken and written about the charismatic movement. In fact it is the church that is the true charismatic movement. The church is a company of gifted men and women. But when that word 'gifted' is used in this context it has a very different flavour from the world's usage of that same word. The gifted man in the world's ratings preens himself on his abilities and welcomes the admiration of others. The gifted Christian, by contrast, recognizes that he is a spiritual pauper lifted from the gutter of sin and enriched by the Spirit of God with gifts that fit him for service. Such an awareness brings humility of spirit. It also evokes a feeling of deep gratitude, which in turn leads to a desire that these gifts, so graciously given, should be used to the full—not to inflate the ego or to stir the admiration of the saints, but simply 'for the common good'.

5

Wisdom and Knowledge

Words are of supreme importance in Christianity. It is true that God's great acts in creation, preservation and redemption are the very foundation of the gospel. Yet those very acts, since they occurred in the past, can only be known to subsequent generations by words that not only record them but explain them. Indeed one must go further than that. The first thing that God did in creation was to speak words (Gen 1:3). When God then sent his Son to save sinners, the Saviour was called 'the Word', so closely did his life, ministry, death and resurrection involve words.

The same is true in Christian experience. How do we become Christians? Paul's answer is plain: 'Faith comes from hearing the message, and the message is heard through the word of Christ' (Rom 10:17). The faith of a Christian is not some induced mystical experience. It is not an emotional upsurge resulting from the impact of the love and friendship of Christians, important though these may be. It is essentially the response of mind and heart and will to words that speak of Jesus Christ. It is no wonder, therefore, that Paul asks questions in Romans 10:14–15: 'How can they believe in the one of whom they

68

have not heard? And how can they hear without someone preaching to them? And how can they preach unless they are sent?'

It is not surprising, then, that words figure so prominently in the gifts of the Spirit. The ministry gifts described in Ephesians 4:11–13 are primarily exercised by means of words, whether in public preaching or personal counselling. So too in those gifts recorded in 1 Corinthians 12 that are for the building up of the church, speech again is supremely important, whether in relation to words spoken to men or of prayer and praise addressed to God.

Paul underlines this significance of words in his introduction to his sustained treatment of spiritual gifts. He reminds the Corinthian believers of the futility of the paganism from which God in his grace had delivered them: 'You know that when you were pagans, somehow or other you were influenced and led astray to dumb idols' (1 Cor 12:2). The absurd emptiness of such worship is linked directly to the total lack of any communications from the idols to whom they had been devoted. In spite of the prayers and sacrifices offered, they had never heard a single word of wisdom or of truth.

Here is an echo of the famous scene on Mount Carmel recorded in 1 Kings 18:16–39. In the conflict to determine whether Jehovah or Baal was the true and living God, the priests of Baal displayed the sheer emptiness of their cult. They called on Baal, they shouted and they slashed themselves in their fanatical zeal. Yet in the terse statement of Scripture: 'There was no response, no-one answered'. Elijah's taunts only emphasized the dumb impotence of the idol. 'Shout louder!' he said . . . 'Perhaps he is deep in thought, or busy, or travelling. Maybe he is sleeping and must be awakened'.

Whether it was the baalim of Canaan, the idols of Corinth, or any product of human hands or imagination, all are dumb because all are lifeless. By sheer contrast, our God is the living God. He is the God who speaks. He is the God who, in answering the prayers of his people, continues to speak. He has spoken in his infallible word in the Scriptures of the Old and New Testament. He continues to speak through the preachers and counsellors whom he equips to make that revelation known. These divinely appointed messengers then use words to apply God's truth to the particular needs of those who need a word from the Lord. Since he is the God of truth, then the words he puts on the lips of his servants today will echo, because they are subject to, the words recorded by the Holy Spirit's impulse in the Scriptures.

It is no surprise, then, that the first two gifts on the list in 1 Corinthians 12 are the message (or word) of wisdom and the word of knowledge. By repeating the phrase Paul emphasizes that both gifts are given by the Holy Spirit and also that they are distinct. They are not the outcome of ordinary natural intelligence that is ours by virtue of our creation. They are not the products of sustained study, acute observation of men and events, or intelligent reflection on past experience. They are similar to the results of such human activity in that they involve thought and issue in words. They are, however, on a different level since they are here presented as supernatural manifestations of the sovereign action of the Holy Spirit.

Perfection of wisdom and knowledge are in God alone. Such is that perfection that his judgements are unsearchable. We are forced to acknowledge the truth of Paul's words, 'Who has known the mind of the Lord? Or who has been his counsellor?' (Rom 11:34). That perfect knowledge and that wisdom were reflected in the first man whom God created in his own image and after his likeness (Gen 1:26–27). It was the greatest human tragedy that, in trying to assert their independence, Adam and Eve disobeyed and suffered the consequences. One fundamental aspect of this judgement was the darkening of their minds as far as the truths of God were concerned. Paul sums it up: 'The god of this age has blinded the minds of unbelievers, so that they cannot see the light of the gospel of the glory of Christ' (2 Cor 4:4).

The miracle of grace that brings such a blinded sinner to Christ begins in an enlightenment of the darkened mind. It is no wonder that Paul speaks of the Christian as 'a new creation' for this initial work of God in salvation is an echo of his initial work in creation: 'For God, who said: "Let light shine out of darkness," made his light shine in our hearts to give us the light of the knowledge of the glory of God in the face of Christ' (2 Cor 4:6). All Christians, therefore, have been enlightened. All have been made 'wise for salvation' (2 Tim 3:15). All have been brought to 'know God' (Gal 4:9).

The fellowship of Christians is thus the community of enlightened ones. Since the Spirit of truth dwells within them they are constantly instructed as they read the Scriptures. So they grow in wisdom and knowledge, and indeed make that growth a major theme in their prayers (Eph 1:17; 3:14–19; Phil 1:9; Col 1:9; Ja 1:5; 2 Peter 3:18). That growth in wisdom and knowledge is also promoted by those whom the Spirit appoints within his church as prophets, pastors and teachers. It is also encouraged by the ministry of those to whom the Spirit has entrusted a special endowment of wisdom and knowledge, leading to the utterance of words that profit the hearers.

Wisdom and knowledge are distinct, though closely related. Thus, the word of wisdom and the word of knowledge are here presented as distinct gifts and are also described as being given to different individuals. We need, therefore, to ask in what sense the two are related, and in what sense they are distinct. To answer those questions it will be helpful to look at the two words in their general usage, before turning to their employment here in a charismatic context.

It is not surprising that when Paul speaks of the wisdom and knowledge of God he puts the two words in that order. Without wisdom knowledge is useless. Indeed, one may go further and say that without wisdom knowledge can be positively dangerous. A doctor, for example, may have specialist knowledge from his medical research of the effects of alcohol on the liver, yet he may drink himself into an early grave. Nuclear scientists have probed the frontiers of knowledge by their discoveries, yet such is human folly that the knowledge that might be used for human benefit is being harnessed for human destruction.

Knowledge is conscious, intelligent awareness of people and of things. Knowledge involves the possession of information about the world around us. Wisdom, however, is the ability to use that knowledge for the right purposes. Wisdom sees not just the facts as they are at the moment, but the goal in view. Wisdom also know the best means to employ to reach that goal.

We can see, therefore, why God's wisdom and knowledge are perfect. He is omniscient. There is nothing hidden from him. There is no point of space and no moment of time of which he is ignorant. There is no being, whether angelic, demonic or human, who is not known perfectly by God. And allied to his complete knowledge is his perfect wisdom. He knows the ultimate goal of his own purposes in creation and redemption. He will ultimately recreate all things to produce a new heaven and a new earth in which righteousness will dwell (2 Pet 3:13, Rev 21:1). He will finally summon all his elect from every nation and tribe and tongue, and perfect them in holiness (Rev 7:9). He will finally put every opposing power beneath his feet (1 Cor 15:25).

Knowing, then, the goal to which all things and all beings are being directed, God also has infinite wisdom so that he uses natural phenomena, the actions of men and women and even the enmity of his foes to accomplish his purposes. Because he is all-wise he is not beset by what, to human eyes, may seem either a set back or very slow progress towards the goal. There is a majestic certainty about God's wisdom: '[He] works out everything in conformity with the purpose of his will . . . for the praise of his glory' (Eph 1:11–12).

When the Christian experiences God's saving grace in the miracle of the new birth he begins to learn truths to which formerly he was a stranger. He acquires a knowledge of God, of the world and of himself where before there was ignorance. Now also, because his eyes are lifted to the horizon of God's purposes for him, for the church and for creation, he begins to reflect God's wisdom as he prays and plans and works. The initial gift of wisdom led him to see the utter folly of sin and to accept God's offer of mercy. Now it leads him on towards realizing the great aim of Christian living, which is to be so conformed to the call of God as to be a glad and willing worker in the realization of the Lord's great purposes.

It is against this background that we must understand these charismata. They are the gifts of the God of all wisdom and knowledge. They are given in order that those who have received them may be able to help and encourage fellow believers. The latter, though already enlightened to experience the wisdom and knowledge common to all the saints, yet need on occasions a special ministry from the Lord.

We are all of us familiar with situations where we need wisdom. We possess the general wisdom that is ours because we are Christians. We study the Scriptures and discover the principles that should guide us in our decisions and choices of appropriate actions. We discover, however, that it is in the area of application that we face the real problem. We may recognize, for example, that the perplexing situation confronting us is similar to that which Christians in Corinth were facing. The principles to guide us are there in Paul's replies to the questions that had come to him from the churches. Yet what he wrote was not a detailed manual of rules and regulations to cover every conceivable issue that might arise. Rather, he addresses them as Christians who have the Holy Spirit dwelling in them. They have just to apply the lessons he teaches in their own personal or domestic situation. While that situation may have general or even basic similarities to our own, there are also special elements. There is the complex tangle that comprises our particular temperament, our family situation and the faith or lack of faith of those involved. So we need wisdom to see how in detail we are to apply the word to our particular issue.

The same kind of question can confront a church. We know from the New Testament how a church is to be constituted and governed. We have the pattern of elders and deacons ministering as we see them ministering in the pastoral epistles. We recognize the truth that each Christian has, through his or her priesthood, direct access to God. We acknowledge that each Christian has wisdom and insight to contribute. Yet still we face thorny problems such as church discipline or co-operation with other congregations in some enterprises, or any other of a variety of matters that demand a right judgement. In short, we face the application of the principles that we all share. Yet it is precisely here that sometimes special wisdom is needed. A two-thirds majority vote may carry the church meeting, yet it is not of necessity the mind of the Lord for the action that needs to be taken.

We are only too familiar with the clarity of hindsight. Those who have not had to make our decision, but have observed subsequently that it was the wrong one, can tell us that very emphatically. We do not, however, need their emphasis since we are all strong in the area of hindsight.

It is foresight that we really need. It is the wisdom that guides us into the future that we need rather than the easy assurance of the post-mortem.

I have emphasized our need of help, whether as individual Christians or as churches, in order to stress that the charismata under discussion are neither substitutes for the Scriptures nor alternatives to prayer and deliberation. All these are basic to our discussion, whether personal or corporate. God, however, has revealed to us that within the fellowship of the church no one is self-sufficient and no leader is all-sufficient. We need one another and we require all the varied ministries and gifts that the Spirit gives. We share together the enlightenment of the Spirit that enables us to grasp the meaning of the Scriptures. Yet we also need the wisdom of our fellow believers.

When Jesus promised his disciples wisdom to face the interrogation by persecutors he was clearly referring to something special. It was not simply a sharpening of their native wits. Nor was it only the spiritual enlightenment that would accompany growing maturity and increasing familiarity with biblical teaching. He spoke, rather, of special situations that would require a quite special understanding.

A law court with skilled interrogators is daunting enough. It is very much worse if the whole legal process is loaded against you and the aim of the judge is not so much to reach a fair verdict as, at all costs, to find the accused guilty. Add to that the fact that often a Christian has had to face such a trial after a period of imprisonment with privations, if not actual torture, and it is abundantly clear that normal reasoning would be insufficient. There would not be time available to give thought to the charges. There would be no possibility of consulting other believers. It is clear, therefore, that the wisdom of which Jesus speaks is a special gift of the Holy Spirit: 'But when they arrest you, do not worry about what to say or how to say it. At that time you will be given what to say, for it will not be you speaking, but the Spirit of your Father speaking through you' (Mt 10:19–20).

The fulfilment of that promise is seen in the Acts. Stephen, full of the Holy Spirit, preached with great authority and did great wonders and miraculous signs. There was powerful opposition, yet, in spite of their arguments, his opponents were worsted. Luke's record gives the reason: 'They could not stand up against his wisdom or the Spirit by which he spoke' (Acts 6:10). One of his bitterest opponents was Saul of Tarsus whose formidable intellectual ability and thoroughgoing Rabbinic training were no match for the divinely-given wisdom of the martyr. Yet that same Saul, humbled and raised up to serve God, was later to show the same gift. In his various court appearances before a wide variety of accusers and judges, he was again and again given 'the word of wisdom'.

When Paul faced the contentious spirit at Corinth that led some Christians to take fellow believers to court, he rebuked them. However, it was not only a negative rebuke that it was wrong to go to law before unbelievers; there was also a positive challenge: 'Is it possible that there is nobody among you wise enough to judge a dispute between believers?' (1 Cor 6:5). Clearly he expects to find in a local church at least one who in such a dispute can give a word of wisdom to which the disputants should give heed.

The wisdom which is here described as a charisma is thus a special enduement. It is, however, not simply wisdom that leads someone to act in a particular way. It is 'an utterance of wisdom'. In other words, it is a statement given by one specifically enlightened by God to point the way forward.

I recall an occasion some years ago when I had been

approached with a view to ministering in a very well-known church. I was greatly drawn to the possibility. There would be a strategic location, or so I thought, for preaching the word. An older and very godly minister was also very warm to the idea. Yet one of my closest friends in the ministry took a totally different view. He wrote to me with a rare note of authority, recalling the sixteenth-century evangelist Farel calling down the curse of heaven on John Calvin if he dared to move from Geneva. I would have been hesitant to go in the face of such a word, backed up as it was not only by the solid arguments he mustered but by the spiritual calibre of the man who used them. I proceeded no further!

If this wisdom, then, is neither natural intuition nor the general wisdom of the mature believer, but rather a special disclosure of the divine wisdom, then the same is true of 'a word of knowledge'. It is not the intuitive discernment of the natural man—what is often referred to as a 'hunch'. Neither is it the knowledge acquired by long experience of life. It is, in the context of Paul's statement, clearly a knowledge supernaturally bestowed.

Peter's encounter with Ananias and Sapphira recorded in Acts 5:1–10 is an illustration of this kind of knowledge bestowed by God in a special situation. It is clear from the narrative that outwardly there was no hint of deception. On the contrary, it seemed to be one more example of the generous and sacrificial generosity that was being displayed among so many of the Jerusalem Christians. Peter's knowledge was manifestly given by God. His reading of the heart and his awareness of the deceitfulness of the couple can only be explained on the grounds that the Holy Spirit, to whom they lied, had revealed the deception to Peter.

A book well known to an earlier generation, *The Scots Worthies*, records some of the stories of the Scottish covenanters. It was a period of intense persecution with the king endeavouring by military repression to impose an Anglican form of worship on a very reluctant people. It records stories of brutality and also of heroism, and among the notable characters in the book is Alexander Peden. He was given—one can only conclude it was by God—a knowledge of specific concern to the persecuted believers. He 'knew', for example, that there would be troops at a certain place on the road and so he could warn folk to keep clear of the danger spot. As he was not privy to army plans, and as he had no means of knowing about troop movement—there were neither electronic surveillance instruments nor telephone communications in the seventeenth century!—one can only conclude that his knowledge was acquired by direct communication from the Lord. His 'words of knowledge' doubtless saved many from imprisonment, torture or death.

It may seem to be a much more mundane affair to turn to a church meeting where a practical problem of some importance is being discussed, or to one of the various thorny issues that can arise in the area of marriage tensions or to the need for guidance in face of a personal decision that has to be made. Yet it is here, in the ongoing life of a local congregation, that someone may be enlightened to see clearly the true issue involved and so be able to lead others to wise action.

To sum up, God himself is the source of all wisdom and knowledge. Christ, in whom reside all the treasures of wisdom and knowledge (Col 2:3), has revealed the mind of God to men and women. The Spirit, having moved men to record that revelation in the Scriptures, now expounds the truth to God's people. He does so through the preaching and teaching ministries that he has given to the church. He also imparts wisdom and knowledge in special situations that call for a specific application of the truths of the word. Because the utterances, whether of wisdom or of knowledge, came from the Spirit of truth, they will never contradict the Scriptures. Indeed, they will be subject to and governed by the Spirit's testimony in the Scriptures. The ultimate aim, whether through the patient study of the Bible, through the public preaching of the word or through Spirit-prompted utterances, is that the people of God might be instructed and equipped to serve with mind and heart.

6

Faith

Faith is the basic Christian response to the grace of God. God has always taken the initiative. He always does, and he always will. Because those whom he approaches are sinners and, therefore, by definition rebels, his approach is totally undeserved. Since judgement and condemnation would be entirely just and appropriate, his condescension, his mercy, his forgiveness and his ready welcome to sinful men and women—all these emerge, not from an attempt on God's part to reward our efforts, but are totally without merit on our side. We are saved by grace alone.

Faith is our response to that grace. Indeed, the more we reflect on our response and the more we examine it in the light of Scripture, so the more we recognize that our response has been graciously elicited by God's grace. So Paul writes, 'By grace you have been saved, through faith —and this not from yourselves, it is the gift of God—not by works, so that no-one can boast' (Eph 2:8–9). Similarly, when Luke describes Lydia's conversion he does not tell of her opening her heart to the Lord. Rather, he writes: 'The Lord opened her heart to respond to Paul's message' (Acts 16:14).

Faith, then, is our response to the overtures of God's

grace. Faith means listening to what God has to say. It is not, however, the listening of the critical observer who weighs up another's words, perhaps to accept, perhaps to qualify, perhaps to reject. Rather, it is the glad listening of one who is hopelessly lost and meets one who clearly knows the route ahead. It is the grateful listening of one who is desperately ill and responds to the assuring words of a highly skilled physician. It is the listening by a condemned criminal to the reading of a royal amnesty.

So faith listens to the word of God in its sobering exposure of sin, and its solemn warnings of judgement. Faith is the assent of the awakened soul to the verdict of the divine judge. And faith continues to listen as the Scriptures speak of the Saviour who came to save those who are lost. Faith says its deep 'Amen' to all that the Scripture has to say about the Saviour who died, the righteous in place of the unrighteous, to bring us to God. Faith is also the 'Hallelujah' of the one who hears God's word speak of the empty tomb and the risen Lord. Faith is the glad acceptance of the promises of forgiveness and new life. Faith is the willing response to the Saviour's invitation, 'Come to me'. Faith is the confidence of being accepted by a welcoming God.

Faith is not simply the response that stands at the threshold of the Christian life. It is certainly true that it is the basic response, so that, having heard and received the good news, we are 'justified by faith' (Rom 5:1 ff.). It is, however, also true that 'We live by faith, not by sight' (2 Cor 5:7), for faith is the necessary element in Christian progress. We began by faith and we must continue by faith. So Paul writes to the Colossians: 'Just as you received Christ Jesus as Lord, continue to live in him, rooted and built up in him, strengthened in the faith as you were taught' (Col 2:6–7). At every stage of the Christian life we must be alert to hear God's word and prompt to obey. That is the life of faith.

This means that faith is not a special qualification of some Christians. It is the common attitude of all. Indeed, without faith we are not Christians at all: 'Without faith it is impossible to please God, because anyone who comes to him must believe that he exists and that he rewards those who earnestly seek him' (Heb 11:6). In the New Testament another title for a non-Christian is an unbeliever. On the positive side the Christian is a believer. It is the most basic element in his or her Christianity.

If, then, faith is so basic to all of us that without it we are not Christians at all, how then can it be described as a charisma? How also can it be presented as a gift that, like other charismata, is graciously given to some believers but not to all? Is this faith some other response? Is it the same word used in some different sense? It is to these questions that we need to address ourselves.

We can surely rule out the idea that faith is being used in some subtly different sense. It is such a fundamental word in the vocabulary of the New Testament, such a basic term in the language of Christian doctrine, that it would be utterly confusing to think that Paul uses it in 1 Corinthians 12:9 in some very different way. It must surely still be what it always is in the Bible, namely, the response of the soul to the word of the Lord. Paul's statement in Romans 10:17 is basic to all our discussion: 'Consequently, faith comes from hearing the message, and the message is heard through the word of Christ'.

There is one further observation. The gift of faith is not to be viewed as faith in its increasingly mature condition. After all, every Christian is summoned to grow spiritually. This means that the childlike confidence of the new believer is intended to develop into the steady trust of the mature man or woman of God. The call to augment faith by spiritual growth that Peter gives in 2 Peter 1:5–8 is addressed to believers in general. Everyone who is in Christ is expected to live the life of faith, and this can never be a stagnant experience.

The gift of faith must, therefore, belong to the same category as the other charismata. It is a special enduement granted by the sovereign Spirit of God in accordance with his own will. The aim, as with the other gifts, is so to enrich one believer that he or she may enrich others; so to equip him or her in a special way that they may function more usefully in the body of Christ. Like the other charismata, faith is given 'for the common good'.

This means that the charisma of faith is of the same essential character as that exercised by every believer in that it is response to the word of God. Yet at the same time it is of a more developed kind. It is especially rich. It is particularly strong. Nor are these 'plus' attributes the result of a diligent use by the believer of the normal means of grace, namely reading the word, listening to the preaching of the word, praying, etc. This faith has such an unusual quality of strength and spiritual daring that one must look for its explanation in a supernatural source. The special ministry of the Spirit is that source!

Two outstanding Christians of the last century may serve as illustrations of this special gift of faith, namely, James Hudson Taylor and George Müller. Hudson Taylor felt the pressures of God upon him to take the gospel to inland China, a vast and unreached area of needy souls. He had, of course, the gospel imperative to take the message to all the nations. He had also the repeated promises of the Scriptures that God would be with him. But how could he venture on such a task with no denominational backing? How could he court the wrath of Victorian society by risking the lives of women missionaries in what his contemporaries must have viewed as a mad venture? The answer was the activity of God's Spirit in his life so that, believing God, he was ready to attempt what was humanly speaking impossible.

He was led to formulate principles that would guide his

successors and inspire a great host of Christians ever since. 'God's work done in God's way will never lack God's supply.' This meant great ventures of faith that were, however, also controlled by the principle of integrity: 'The China Inland Mission will not knowingly incur debt.' These, and the other financial guidelines, emerged out of the depths of God's dealings with him in the inner recesses of his soul.

His aim was not to make a name for himself. Nor had he any interest in a radical approach to missions for its own sake. He wanted to see Chinese brought to Christ and churches established. God who called him also equipped him. The charisma of faith was with Hudson Taylor a singularly fruitful gift, the consequences of which are seen still in China today.

George Müller of Bristol was of a similar stamp. Again there was a very worthy aim in view, that is, the rescue of destitute children from the misery and moral dangers in which the nineteenth century specialized. The realization of that aim was again a seemingly impossible goal in view of his total lack of resources. His method to many a hard-headed financier must have seemed almost criminally foolish. Faced with the urgent daily necessity of feeding and clothing hundreds of orphans who were totally dependent on him, he never explicitly nor indirectly brought the needs before men. He looked in faith directly to his heavenly benefactor who never failed him.

Müller, in fact, had an aim that transcended even that of caring for his orphan children. In the face of an unbelieving age in which even within the churches liberal theology was trying to jettison the supernatural, Müller wanted to demonstrate that there is a living God who hears prayer and meets his people's needs when they cry to him.

Neither Hudson Taylor nor George Müller were spiritual cranks engaged in off-beat enterprises. Nor were they insisting that every Christian charity or society must be run on their lines. They believed God had called them to their particular ministries. They believed that God had summoned them in order to demonstrate his power, his wisdom and his provision for every need. The faith that enabled them to scale these lofty peaks of spiritual endeavour and achievement was itself a supernatural gift. It was the charisma of faith.

One of the many missionaries who later went to China with the China Inland Mission was James Frazer. God gave him a deep concern for the Lisu people in the mountains of south-west China. They were difficult to reach physically because of the mountainous terrain where their villages clung to the high slopes. They were even more difficult to reach spiritually—Satan does not easily relinquish an area where he has been dominant for so long. Frazer prayed as any pioneer in such a situation would pray. He also had a power base back home. This was not simply the large group of general supporters. It comprised a small number of people who were as committed to the evangelization of Lisuland as was Frazer. Together they prayed while he toiled on with his evangelistic work.

There came a point, however, when God gave him such an assurance of answered prayer that he began to praise God. He had not yet seen the Lisu begin to turn to Christ as later they would do in their thousands. It would be more correct to say that he had not seen them with the normal sight of his eyes. However, the eye of faith had been opened by the Spirit of God. His was not the kind of praise that is sometimes advocated today when someone is urged to start praising for answered prayer. That kind of response can be simply a dutiful performance of what is prescribed rather than a true response. It can, as a result, lead to disillusionment when the answer for which praise has already been offered does not materialize.

Frazer's faith was not some kind of intensified wishful thinking. It was not belief screwed up by his persistent praying. Rather, it was a charisma, a gift of the Spirit. Because of the one who gave him the faith to believe that God had heard him, his praise was in fact the Spirit-given response to the Spirit-given assurance. This is the faith that can remove mountains!

Lest some should feel that such faith is granted only to great pioneers or preachers, it is important to recognize that God may grant that same charisma to one who, in the popular parlance, would be described as an ordinary church member. I recall a visit to a small chapel in Yorkshire where I heard testimony to a woman of faith. The chapel had fallen on evil days and the congregation was reduced to one old lady. Common sense would have indicated that sadly it was time to call it a day, turn the key in the lock and consign the building, like so many others, to decay or to some other use. However, God had given her an assurance that he still had a purpose for that place. Thus, Sunday by Sunday, she would go and open up the chapel, even though normally she was the entire congregation.

To the unbelievers it must have seemed either pathetic or distinctly odd. In fact it was neither! She had the gift of faith that enabled her to persist. When I preached there in 1982 the old lady had gone to glory, but the vision had been realized. There was the congregation with its pastor and its evident life and blessing. The faith that sees such marvellous tokens of God's blessing is not the exclusive possession of the great Christians whose biographies are on our shelves. It is the gift that God gives again and again to Christians in a local congregation.

One other area where this distinctive faith is often manifested is within the life of a family. Parents have a great delight in seeing their children grow up to serve the God of their father and mother. On the other hand, they are deeply pained when one of their children turns his or her back on the gospel. There are times, however, when God has been pleased to give the gift of faith to a parent.

They may not see the hoped-for conversion of son or daughter for many years. Indeed, they may die and leave behind one who is still an unbeliever. Yet, where God has given such a faith, it not only leads to a great assurance in the heart of the parent who prays, it also leads in God's time to his sovereign work. The faith that held on in the face of long-deferred hope is, after all, the response of the heart to the word spoken deep within by the Lord, that in due time the unbelieving one will be truly born again.

Such accounts can elicit questions from Christians who are struggling against great problems. The lonely missionary, the member of a seemingly dying congregation, the troubled parent—all of them may object that such testimonies tend to deepen their own personal gloom of soul. But the contrary should be the case. This gift, like all the others, is 'for the common good'. It is not granted to one Christian in order to bring comfort and joy to one individual. Nor is it given to plunge others into dejection. Rather, it is given in order to stimulate all of us. All of us have the Spirit within. All of us have the promises of the word. God calls us to believe his word and to pray on. He also raises up men and women to whom he grants an especial measure of faith in order to challenge, stimulate and indeed encourage all of us. They are his trail-blazers in the life of faith. Like any pioneer they are prominent. But like any pioneer they also summon those who follow to press on along the same path.

'Now faith is the substance of things hoped for, the evidence of things not seen' (Heb 11:1 AV). Thus the roll of honour of the spiritual leaders of the Old Testament is introduced. Faith reaches into the future and makes the future present. Faith reaches into the unseen realm and makes what is hidden visible. Faith is so vividly aware that what God has promised he must perform that it treats future events as being as firm as present happenings. Faith sees the realm of God's spiritual dealings not as some slightly unreal condition of things but rather as real as, if not more real than, the changing pattern of life in front of our eyes. The spiritual giants of the Old Testament were 'strong in faith'. In spite of the fact that they faced danger, persecution and discouragement, they still believed God. Although the full dawning of the gospel was still historically on the far horizon, they lived and suffered and died in the assurance of membership in a kingdom that nothing could shake.

This spiritual roll of honour was included, not for antiquarian reasons, but with the definite aim of stimulating us to action now. The 'great cloud of witnesses' declares a faith that can face impossible odds and still triumph. The Christian now is the heir of the saints of the Old Testament. The spiritual pioneers of that era, the period of the preparatory covenant, are presented as a challenge to us to persist in the life of faith.

This pioneer and challenging role leads the author to turn to the even greater stimulus. It comes from Jesus himself, the Messiah whose coming the Old Testament saints anticipated. He is described as 'the author [or pioneer] and perfecter of our faith' (Heb 12:2). He has gone before. In the imagery of Hebrews 12, drawn as it is from the Greek athletic arena, Jesus is already at the end of the course. Having displayed faith in all its perfection and completeness, he summons us to follow. For him faith reached into glory and in face of the suffering of Cavalry he saw the joy set before him and used it as if it had been already realized in order to support his struggle on the cross.

No Christian, however mature, will ever stand in the same position of eminence as Jesus. Yet by the gift of his

Spirit he has entrusted ministries to the members of his body, the church. Thus the gift of faith enables a Christian in some measure to reflect the great 'author and perfecter of faith'. While Jesus is the pre-eminent one in his glorious exaltation, yet he condescends to his people by endowing some of them with a faith that challenges the rest. As pioneers they reflect the great forerunner himself. Being 'strong in faith' they stimulate others to press on and to look always to Jesus.

7

Miraculous Healing?

There is scarcely anything more calculated to stir interest than the announcement of a healing meeting. A healing crusade is even more likely to arouse attention. It is not only that there are many whose curiosity stirs them to respond to anything out of the ordinary. There are also those whose interest is linked to their own illness or the sickness of someone within the family circle or of some close friend. Naturally they want to see if people really are being healed. Their interest is not merely theoretical. Healing is to them a matter of great, if not desperately urgent, importance.

Some Christian leaders will gladly respond to this kind of reaction. They would dismiss the suggestion that they are using possible healing as a kind of bait to draw those who are totally uninterested in the gospel. Indeed, they would argue that it is both legitimate and biblical to expect healings, and to anticipate also their drawing power. After all, they would argue, was it not the fact of Jesus' healing ministry that led to the influx of the crowds to hear his preaching?

It often seems to escape notice, however, that Jesus never organized healing crusades. Nor did he ever invite people to come and see the healings that were going to be performed. He did not specify in advance what sicknesses would be healed. Indeed he reacted in quite the contrary fashion to the readiness to flock to where healings had taken place. So the arrival of the curious crowds led, not to a further display of his power, but to his exodus from the scene (Mk 3:7–12).

When he proved that his power was absolute and could call a child back from death itself, he refused the obvious possibility of drawing the crowds. Indeed, he gave strict instructions to the family 'not to let anyone know about this' (Mk 5:43). His mercy and his power were irresistible, but publicity was totally rejected. When he pointed to his healings as a demonstration that he was the Messiah, it was not the crowds nor the religious leaders whom he was trying to convince. Rather, it was a gracious reassurance to a believer racked by doubts and questions, John the Baptist (Mt 11:2–5).

The argument that an appeal to signs and wonders is the way to commend the gospel to men has to face the story Jesus himself told of the rich but ungodly man and the godly beggar (Lk 16:19–31). It was the wisdom of hell that led the rich man after his death to appeal to heaven for the raising to life of the poor man. Surely, if Lazarus was restored to life such a stupendous miracle would stir his own surviving brothers to repentance, and so to the avoidance of his own place of torment. However, the reply from heaven, in Jesus' story, is quite clear: 'They have Moses and the Prophets; let them listen to them' (Lk 16:29).

The pleading continues with a remarkably twentieth-century emphasis. They will not listen to preaching and they will not read the Bible, but if someone returns from the dead they will repent. The answer from heaven is timeless, and is as incisive today as when Jesus first spoke it: 'If they do not listen to Moses and the Prophets, they will not be convinced even if someone rises from the dead' (Lk 16:31).

This is not to deny that the New Testament gives abundant evidence that people were awakened and led to repentance as a consequence of seeing or being themselves the recipients of miraculous healing. Nor does it ignore the fact that when questions are prompted because of the impact of a miracle an answer was given. Jesus was ready to reply to the criticism of the religious leaders when he healed on the Sabbath (Lk 13:15–16). He was prepared to reinforce his healing miracles with a warning, and a call to repentance and holiness of life (Jn 5:14). Peter was similarly ready to answer the leaders in Jerusalem when they questioned him about the healing of the lame man. Indeed, he went further and used it to press home a warning of God's judgement, and a summons to repent (Acts 3:12; 4:8f). Yet, while gladly utilizing the occasion to present the gospel, they never laid on the healing miracles as a pre-evangelism effort to arouse interest.

Far from seeing signs and wonders as the great stimulus to faith, Jesus took an entirely different position. His words and the claims he made were the primary grounds for responding to him in faith. In fact, he puts the appeal to the evidence drawn from his miracles as very much secondary. It sounds like a concession to those whose weak faith finds it hard to accept his words. So he says, 'Believe me when I say that I am in the Father and the Father is in me; or at least believe on the evidence of the miracles themselves' (Jn 14:11).

Some further cautionary words are needed in view of some misplaced claims to healing miracles, and the further claim that such healings authenticate the agent as being truly sent by God. In reply to the latter, it is important to remember that remarkable healings have been experienced where there is no commitment at all to the gospel. I recall years ago a great healing crusade in the Royal Albert Hall. Striking phenomena were manifest as people threw away sticks, and claims were made of astonishing miracles. Yet the man who led the meetings was quite explicit in attributing the healings to 'the spirit doctors on the other side'. Demonic activity can mimic divine activity, witness the magicians of Egypt who were able to produce signs and wonders that matched some, at least, of those performed by Moses. Satan will not worry unduly if one of his dupes enjoys a measure of new health if only he ensures that his victim will go to hell.

Jesus spoke clearly on the subject. In a prophecy that needs to be sounded like a trumpet blast to Christians today, he foretold the sorry accompaniment of spiritual decline: 'For false Christs and false prophets will appear and perform great signs and miracles to deceive even the elect—if that were possible.' To a generation that seems ready to let credulity take over, his final word needs to be heard: 'See, I have told you ahead of time' (Mt 24:24–25).

We must also make allowance for faulty diagnosis. It is strange that doctors may be almost decried as agents of healing, and yet are extolled as if they were infallible in the area of diagnosis. Thus, if a doctor has diagnosed cancer, then cancer it must be! A healing is therefore represented as a miraculous victory over the dreaded enemy. The diagnosis may indeed be correct, and the healing miraculous. But we must at least take into account the possibility that the diagnosis was faulty. Ask any doctor and you will be told that diagnosis is in fact often the major problem. An honest doctor is too aware of mistaken assessments in this matter to accept easily the ascription of infallibility!

The late Dr Lloyd-Jones had an experience of this very thing.[7] In 1928 when preaching in south Wales he stayed with an old lady who asked him as a favour to come and preach at the chapel in a year's time. When he agreed, she pushed it further and asked him to come every year until the death of one or other of them. Fresh as he was then from his brilliant medical career he felt safe in his assessment of her health and dubious expectation of life. He agreed to come but found that his diagnosis was faulty, and he was still committed to an annual visit until war broke out in 1939!

Another important consideration is the psychosomatic factor. A deep persuasion of mind or an intensely strong desire can lead to remarkable physical effects, just as, on the other hand, worry or tension can lead to physical conditions such as an ulcer. Dr Lloyd-Jones' old lady gave a further illustration here. Ten years after he had succumbed to her persuasive powers, she was very seriously ill, and in fact the family was told the end was near. The night nurse on duty was surprised to be asked for a calendar, but wanting to humour the old lady in her dying hours she got her one. The comment probably surprised her even more: 'He'll be here in six weeks.' From that point the dying woman made a steady recovery and the doctor was back again at the chapel.

It is this powerful influence of the mind over the body that explains some of the remarkable healings at Lourdes. The anticipation has been built up over the months while the pilgrims are getting ready to travel. The intense expectation, the darkened approach and then the brightly lit grotto—all this can have a profound psychological effect. It is perhaps no surprise that atheist doctors in France, who would reject any notion of the supernatural, will still send some of their patients to Lourdes.

Two other factors should be mentioned. There is the unexplained arrest of a pathological condition. For some reason that doctors cannot explain, the apparent development of a cancer goes into remission, and the patient recovers. Then also there is the well-attested evidence of the consequences of physical or emotional shock. Someone with impairment of speech or hearing is suddenly involved in some traumatic experience and is remarkably restored to normal functioning.

It might seem as if all these cautionary words lead inevitably to the conclusion that miraculous healing can be explained away. That, however, is not the conclusion of the author of this book! My aim, rather, has been to recognize not only the spurious claims, but also those that are fully explicable on natural grounds. It is also with a view to avoiding any kind of approach that will make it more likely that the spurious will be foisted on the Christian public, or the natural and ordinary will be puffed up to be paraded as the supernatural. I am fully persuaded that God heals, not only indirectly by means of medical and nursing care, but also directly by his own immediate action. The skill of the physician or the surgeon is from God our Creator, even if they do not acknowledge the source of their ability. Sometimes, however, God dispenses with his normal agencies, and touches the body of a sick person directly and heals him.

This means that we will want to avoid at all costs inducing an attitude of mind, or conditioning people emotionally. The total absence in the New Testament of special healing meetings is especially significant here. There is no encouragement of feverish excitement, no build up of the atmosphere of a meeting, no conditioning of the audience to anticipate the unusual. The absence of all this does not mean the absence of miracles. But it does mean that when healings take place they are decisively achieved. There are no half-healings, no apparent recoveries that lead to a speedy relapse. Rather, there is healing that is immediate and total.

Allied to this is the assurance with which healing is pronounced. Neither Jesus nor his apostles make tentative claims. There is no hint of hesitation or uncertainty. They do not speak of a hoped-for healing. Where there is not going to be a healing, they neither speak nor act. So, at the pool of Bethesda, Jesus passed crowds of sick folk whom he did not attempt to heal. He went directly to the crippled man who at once was fully restored.

Similarly, Paul did not claim healing for Timothy. Clearly he had no mandate from the Spirit to do this. So he urged a normal medicinal remedy for a chronic stomach condition: 'Stop drinking only water, and use a little wine because of your stomach and your frequent illnesses' (1 Tim 5:23). When he left Trophimus sick in Miletus (2 Tim 4:20), it was not an apostolic failure. It was simply that he did not have the authority from the Holy Spirit to claim healing for his friend, much as he must have desired it. Yet on other occasions, as at Lystra (Acts 14:8–10) and in the case of the official in Malta (Acts 28:7–10), he expected and saw immediate healing.

This area of apparent failure, which was not failure at all but only restraint, points to a very important pastoral issue. To claim healing or to assure a person that the healing has taken place can be quite disastrous if, in fact, there is no healing. The sufferer then has his wretchedness compounded, for he faces not only his pain and sickness, but the feeling of guilt that somehow he has not risen to the demands of faith.

The needs of the bereaved also have to be borne in mind. There is the natural grief over the death of a loved one. If, however, there is a feeling of having failed that loved one by not exercising sufficient faith on their behalf, then their grief will be all the more intensified. The healings of the New Testament avoid this kind of cruelty. When claims to healing are made, they are validated by actual results. When those results are not going to be seen, then claims are not made. Much additional sorrow and distress would be avoided today if a like restraint was shown.

There is a further grave factor bearing on this issue,

though, in fact, it has wider application. To speak with assurance of healing is to assume at that point a prophetic role, for a prediction is being made about the future, namely that the sickness will go. But if the confident prediction is misplaced, an extremely serious indictment faces the one who so confidently made that prediction. It will not do to shrug the shoulders apologetically and admit a mistaken statement. That might be sufficient if we had simply been putting forward our hope for a recovery. The assurance of healing, however, goes further than that. It implies that it is God who has spoken since he alone can make the future known, for to him alone it is an open book.

According to Deuteronomy 18:19–22, the man who speaks with this kind of assurance and whose prediction is falsified by the events faces divine rejection. The verdict is that he has spoken presumptuously, and God did not send him. The death sentence then to be carried out points with solemnity to an equivalent church decision now, namely, suspension from fellowship, and from the Lord's table, and the discrediting of the one who laid claim to a God-given knowledge of the future.

Turning to the positive biblical evidence for God's readiness to heal directly, it is noticeable that the Old Testament does not furnish many examples. Frost pointed out in his book on miraculous healing that of the fifty miracles recorded in the Old Testament, only three apart from the specially significant one associated with the brazen serpent had to do with healing of the body.[8]

Some may point to the title that God revealed in Exodus 15:25–26. He is Jahweh Rophecha, 'the LORD who heals you'. The assurance that none of the diseases of Egypt would affect them is cited as further evidence of God's concern with their bodily health. It must, however, be remembered that this was in the context of God's dealings with his people in the period of what Paul described as their infancy (Gal 4:1–7). Thus, blessings and judgements were alike presented in external terms. On the one side, there are long life, peaceful days and good harvests; on the other hand, judgements are plague, pestilence, famine and the sword of the invader. This same use of the external is seen in the law of ceremonial cleanness and impurity and in the dietary restriction on eating what is ritually unclean. God used the external picture language to teach spiritual truths. Hence, when in the New Testament the emphasis is on the inward and the spiritual, the ceremonial law is abrogated and the health of the soul is seen as being of far greater importance.

It is also good to remember that God's actions in the area of the miraculous were not only linked to periods of revelation, or of conflict with idolatry, but were also quite obviously at certain points tied to a particular stage of Israel's history. Thus, for example, the preservation of clothes and footwear from normal wear and tear (Deut 29:5) and the provision of food via the manna and the quails (Ex 16:11–18) were alike temporary. The entry into Canaan ended this condition of supernatural provision.

Having made these provisos with regard to undue emphasis on, or distortion of, the biblical evidence, it is necessary to note that God certainly did display his power in the area of healing and even of raising from the dead. So Naaman's leprosy was miraculously healed. Hezekiah's boil was cured, though in this case the healing and restoration led to a disastrous subsequent failure. It is a reminder not only that health is not necessarily the supreme good, but that it is a gift that must be handled with great care. In this issue the general principle certainly applied: 'From the one who has been entrusted with much, much more will be asked' (Lk 12:48).

There is, however, one Old Testament passage that is

particularly noteworthy in that it is quoted by Matthew by way of explanation of the significance of the healing ministry of Jesus. The divine purpose of the healing miracles was to fulfil the word of the Lord that had come through Isaiah: 'He took up our infirmities and carried our diseases' (Mt 8:17). The reference is to one of the prophecies that pointed to the suffering servant of the Lord and which Christians have always found to be so vividly prophetic of Jesus' sufferings and death (Is 53:4).

One way of interpreting this statement in Isaiah is summed up in the claim that there is healing in the atonement. The argument is thus presented in terms of conclusions to be drawn as to our hopes of healing or indeed our claim to healing. If Jesus not only bore our sins but bore also our sickness then surely, so the argument runs, just as we may claim the forgiveness of sins on the basis of his atoning work, so also we may claim healing. The inevitable conclusion of this line of argument is to make faith the key element. If we are justified by faith then we may also be healed by faith.

A dark shadow, however, lies across any continued sickness. It is the necessary admission that there must have been a failure of faith. But is the chain of argument and implications valid? In what sense is there healing in the atonement? We need to go back to a more careful scrutiny both of Isaiah's statement and of the use that Matthew makes of it.

It will not do to try and reject the argument by claiming that since the fulfilment of Isaiah's prophecy is linked with Jesus' healing ministry rather than his death, it has no reference to the atonement but only to Jesus' compassion and healing work. For one thing, verse 4 of Isaiah 53 cannot be isolated from the passage of which it is one element. The entire chapter is concerned with the sufferings of the sin-bearer who takes upon himself the penal consequences of his people's transgressions. His substitutionary atonement is the theme of the whole passage.

Then again, it is arbitrary to separate the compassion of Jesus and the signs and wonders of his ministry on the one hand, and his atoning death on the other. His death as a sacrifice for sins only had value because of who he was. But his uniqueness as the God-man who alone could span the gulf brought by sin was declared and authenticated by the signs and wonders of his earlier ministry, and by the supreme sign that was to follow, namely, his resurrection.

In addition to these considerations is the further fact that Jesus himself did not draw a sharp distinction between the forgiveness of sins and the healing of sickness. Thus, in the healing of the palsied man he linked the two together: 'That you may know that the Son of man has authority on earth to forgive sins. . . . Then he said to the paralytic, "Get up, take your mat and go home"' (Mt 9:6). Similarly, in dealing with the woman suffering from a spinal deformity he referred to her as 'a daughter of Abraham'—and that means one of God's covenant people—whom Satan had bound (Lk 13:16).

Coming, then, to a more detailed examination of Isaiah 53:4, it is clear that it is closely linked both to the verse that precedes and to the two verses that follow. Verse 3 speaks of the contempt that he received and the misunderstanding even of his friends and disciples. Verse 4 begins with the emphatic 'surely' (the Hebrew word is *abhen*). It is an explanation of the reason for the misunderstanding, in that all that was seen superficially was his suffering and rejection. Yet, it fact, this suffering was his loving and purposeful bearing of our sins. This close parallel of verses 3 and 4 may be seen if the words are set opposite each other thus:

verse 3a a man of sorrows   verse 4b he carried our
                                    sorrows

| verse 3b acquainted with | verse 4a he carried our |
| sickness | sickness |

Furthermore, the word used, *nasa* ('he bore'), is used also in verse 12 of bearing our sins, this latter verse being quoted in 1 Peter 2:24. It was the word used in the levitical ritual on the day of Atonement for the goat that symbolically bore away the sins of the people. It is not therefore surprising that the Septuagint, the Greek translation of the Old Testament, translated verse 3, 'He bears our sins and suffers pain for us', all of which suggests that the bearing of the sicknesses and the pains was part of his atoning work. For the outside observer, his sufferings could have invited contempt, as indeed they did for the mocking crowd who scoffed at Jesus in his dying agony on the cross. It is only when we see them in the context of his atoning work that they make sense.

Thus Jesus, the suffering servant of the Lord, bore our guilt and our liability to condemnation, and at the same time bore our sicknesses, which are the outward evidence of our fallen state. This is spelt out in precise detail in verse 5, which speaks prophetically of his wounding for our transgressions and his bruising for our iniquities. In short, the atonement wrought by Christ not only met the basic need of fallen humanity, namely, our sinful alienation from God, but also dealt ultimately with all the consequences that flowed from Adam's sin. That is why the cross not only had implications in the area of personal sin, but had further reference to sickness and death, and indeed had cosmic significance in that it purchased the deliverance of the created order from the sorry entail of the fall. In short, the atonement not only paid the price of the believer's justification, but also ensured ultimately the resurrection of the body, and the restoration of all things in a new heaven and a new earth in which righteousness will dwell (2 Pet 3:13; Rev 21:1 ff.).

To return to Matthew 8:17, the infirmities and

diseases that he bore are the evidence of our fallen state. The compassion he showed and the power he displayed in his healing miracles were both an authentication of his claims to be the suffering servant of Israel's prophecy, and also a foreshadowing of his atoning death for our sins, and for all their consequences. His miracles of healing were thus not only works of compassion, but testimonies to his divine nature and mission (see Mt 11:2–5; Jn 20:31).

To sum up the argument, in Matthew 8:17 we see Jesus healing by virtue of his coming death. He was also able to forgive sins during his ministry prior to his death because of the atonement that was yet in the future, but was viewed by God as an accomplished reality. So also he was able to heal the sicknesses and diseases that were the outcome of sin by virtue of the sacrifice for sin that he would soon make at Calvary. Because he was the sin-bearer at the cross, he was also the bearer of all the consequences of sin. The forgiveness and new life he imparts now are the fruit of his atonement and also a foretaste of the coming glory of heaven.

This acknowledgement that there is healing in the atonement does not, however, lead necessarily to the conclusion that by faith we may claim healing in the same way as we claim forgiveness by faith. After all, while it is true that Jesus bore our sins in his own body on the tree (1 Pet 2:24), that does not lead us to assume that sinless perfection is available to us here and now. Some have indeed claimed this position, but apart from the weight of scriptural evidence against them, experience has sadly demonstrated that such perfection belongs only to heaven where sin will be finally and for ever banished. Here we certainly reap the first fruits of Christ's death in that God freely forgives us and reconciles us to himself. The remission of guilt and the acceptance of the justified sinner are alike final. Yet the struggle with indwelling sin continues. In Luther's vivid phrase we are *simul justus ac peccator* ('at once justified and a sinner'). The pledge, however, is absolutely sure, that God will one day complete the saving work in each one of his people. Grace now in justification points forward with certainty to glory then!

Similarly, the bearing of our sicknesses at Calvary is the basis of the biblical vision of heaven in which God 'Will wipe every tear from their eyes. There will be no more death or mourning or crying or pain, for the old order of things has passed away' (Rev 21:4). We can no more avoid sickness here than we can avoid death. Yet neither hold the menace they once posed. Whatever the ravages of disease that may afflict our bodies, here it is but a temporary trial for our resurrection bodies will be immune. However ugly death may appear in its coming and its accompaniments, its sting has been drawn. At the very moment when death seems triumphantly to claim its victim, it loses him or her for ever. Death is swallowed up in victory (1 Cor 15:54).

While, however, we must not foster unbiblical expectation of perfect health, we must not go to the other extreme and expect no alleviation of our present position. While the New Testament never promises healing on every occasion to the believer, it does not leave us without any hope at all of divine intervention in our sicknesses. The miracles of the Acts and the experience of countless Christians since then point to the reality of supernatural healing.

It may be helpful to pursue the analogy of the Redeemer's dealing with our sins. While it is true that he does not promise us sinless perfection, it is also abundantly clear that he does not leave his reconciled people to flounder in their indwelling sinfulness. There is a constant summons to holiness. There are also promises of power. So the Christian is to expect a deepening experience of the Lord's deliverance in the battle with indwelling sin. We are not on a spiritual see-saw all the way through our Christian lives. Rather, we are expected to mature and to make progress. So, while sinless perfection is the goal that will only be attained in heaven, we are given gracious foregleams of that coming glory. John Newton put it so well:

> I am not what I ought to be. I am not what I want to be. I am not what I hope to be. But, blessed be God, I am not what once I was, and by the grace of God I am what I am.

Let me apply the analogy to the issue of sickness. While the total healing of our bodies purchased by Christ's atonement still awaits the final day of glory, there are bright foregleams of that glory. So the Lord, for his own gracious ends, may leave Paul to struggle with his thorn in the flesh, while giving him grace to endure. Yet he may also use that same Paul to effect cures that can only be explained as evidence of the miracle-working power of God. The continuing pains of the saints are the reminder that the full glory of the resurrection of the body is always still ahead. The supernatural healings that the Lord graciously performs are not only tokens of his love and his power, but are themselves powerful prophecies of what he will finally do. It is this positive side of healing we turn to in the next chapter.

8

When God Truly Heals

If the cautionary thrust of the previous chapter was that God does not always heal, the confident emphasis of this present chapter is that he *does* still heal, not only indirectly by medical means, but also by his own direct action. Two passages of Scripture require particular attention: Paul's list of spiritual gifts in 1 Corinthians 12 and James' teaching about the role of the elders in the ministry of healing.

What is so striking about Paul's reference in 1 Corinthians 12:9 is that he does not speak, as he is often popularly misquoted, about 'the gift of healing'. He speaks, rather, of 'gifts of healings', using the plural. The plural of the word charisma is used here; it is charismata that are bestowed by the Holy Spirit as he equips Christians to serve their fellows. So too, it is not the word 'healing' that is used here (in the Greek) but the plural 'healings'. The phrase may thus be translated literally as 'gifts that lead to healings'.

It is clear that Paul is speaking here in the context of the Holy Spirit's activity within the church. The theme of the passage is that the Holy Spirit is sovereign in allocating his gifts. He gives them to those whom he chooses in order to bring a contribution of service to the church and so glorify the Lord. This means that ministries in the area of healing do not belong to every Christian but to those to whom the Spirit, in his unexplained sovereignty, chooses to give them. What is not so clear is why the 'gifts of healings' should be represented in the plural. We may be quite firm in asserting that there are spiritually endowed members of the body of Christ who are supernaturally equipped to minister healing to others. Where, I believe, I must be much more tentative is in spelling out precisely why, both in verse 9 and again in verse 28 and 30, Paul uses the plural.

One suggestion is that the gifts of healing are distributed in such a way that different people have different diseases where they are able to effect healing. One can only say of this that it is a possible inference, but there is no evidence elsewhere in the New Testament to support it. There is no hint in Acts 2 that Peter specialized in healings of the lower limbs, nor that Paul concentrated on fevers! When Jesus promised his disciples, 'I tell you the truth, anyone who has faith in me will do what I have been doing. He will do even greater things than these' (Jn 14:12), he spoke as one who went about 'healing every disease and sickness' (Mt 4:23).

It would seem to fit the wider New Testament context to suggest that 'the healings' in view are, in fact, a very diverse ministry. There is not only sickness of the body but sickness of the mind. Indeed, sometimes it is the latter that leads to the former—persistent mental tension or distress can lead to bodily sickness. Then again, there is the area of broken relationships that can produce physical symptons—a family dispute can lead to a stomach ulcer!

Healing is thus not simply dealing with a physical state but with various causes and effects that are often interrelated in ways that may not be apparent, even to the skilled physician. I recall a father and son who were in a state of open hostility; and were both receiving medical treatment for stomach trouble. The pity was that they were patients of different doctors, neither of whom, naturally, was in a position to know where the real seat of the trouble was, and where healing was primarily required.

This may possibly be an explanation of the use of the plural 'healings', but what about the fact that 'gifts' also appear as a plural? It will not do to say that it is because they are given to a number of people, for that applies to other gifts as well. Indeed, that interpretation is ruled out by the context. In listing the various charismata Paul speaks of then being allocated by the Spirit 'to each one ... to one ... to another ... to another ... to still another'. In each case the individual recipient is in view, though obviously he or she belongs to a larger group. So in the case of 'the gifts of healings' it is still one individual who has these gifts.

This also, incidentally, rules out the first suggested interpretation of some kind of specializing in one area of healing. The plain inference to be drawn from the context is that each particular individual to whom the Spirit imparts this ministry receives not a gift to be exercised in one direction, but gifts that are to be utilized in all the varied healings that the sovereign Spirit chooses to bestow.

I would suggest another possible interpretation. It is that the reference is not to 'a gift' that is a permanent endowment but to 'gifts' that are bestowed on particular occasions, and for specific purposes. It is one thing to envisage someone with a 'gift of healing' who would continue to employ the gift in all the frequent encounters with illness that arise, or whenever some healing meeting or crusade is planned. It is quite another to have in view someone who does not have the ability permanently to hand, but is supernaturally equipped on each particular occasion. Such gifts would be occasional, and indeed might even be very rarely used.

This would account for the fact that while the record of the Acts points to a continuing employment of evangelistic and pastoral gifts, for example, it only occasionally refers to healings. That they truly happened is quite clear. That they did not happen all the time is equally clear. That there could be a season of special manifestation, as when Peter's shadow brought healing, is also clear (Acts 5: 15–16). In a similarly unusual time of special divine visitation, the narrative (Acts 19:11–12) emphasizes that the miracles wrought were extraordinary. Since every miracle is, by definition, extraordinary the quite unusual feature of these healings was their abundance, and the strangeness of the instrument employed, namely, hand-kerchiefs or aprons that had been in contact with the apostle.

This interpretation of 'gifts of healings' as being special endowments of supernatural healing power for specific use also fits in with what we have noted earlier about the decisiveness of the apostolic healings. They not only knew when there would be healings, but when there would not be healings. Unlike the gift of tongues, for example, which could be used or silenced at will (1 Cor 14:28), the gifts of healings were used only as the Spirit prompted, and with that prompting to act or to speak there was clearly an accompanying assurance. Peter at the temple gate not only knew that healing would occur—hence his authoritative word—but clearly was the agent endowed at that precise point with healing power.

When we turn to James 5:13–16 we are moving in the area of developed church life. If we compare the arrangements to deal with the distribution of alms in Acts 6 and the precise and detailed instruction about elders and deacons in the pastoral epistles, we can see that in the revelation of God's purposes for his church there is progress. Thus the letter of James reflects a settled church order in which a body of elders constitutes the oversight of the flock. Their authority is indicated by the title 'elder' and their pastoral concern by their title 'overseer' ('bishop' in the Authorized Version). They are thus not only responsible for the right government of the local church, but also for the personal pastoral oversight of the members.

It is against this background of a divinely authorized pastoral team that we are to understand James' instructions to the sick to send for the elders. The great shepherd is now in heaven at the right hand of power. The under-shepherds are therefore appointed to minister in his name and with his compassion. It is to this pastoral body rather than simply to one of the team to whom the sick person is to apply.

It is important to notice, and indeed to stress, that the initiative is to come from the sick person. It is not that the elders are to take the first step. Of course they are to be available and that means that the teaching and preaching in the congregation will make it clear that they are available. It is, however, the sick person himself who is required to make the initial approach.

The steps to be taken are clearly presented. They are 'to pray over him'. This implies not only the literal position of those who may be around a sick person lying in bed, but also the prayer directed specifically towards the sick person and his immediate needs. They are also to anoint him with oil. This would seem to have a twofold reference. Oil with its soothing effects was a widespread agent in general care for the sick. In the story of the good Samaritan, he not only uses wine as an antiseptic but oil as a healing balm. Similarly in the familiar pastoral setting of Psalm 23 the Shepherd anoints the fevered or bruised head of the sheep with oil.

There is, however, a further reference. In the Old

Testament the prophet, priest and king were all anointed, but the anointing was a spiritual unction as they were set apart by the Holy Spirit for their ministry. This is spelled out by Isaiah in words that the Messiah was later to apply to himself: 'The Spirit of the Sovereign LORD is on me, because the LORD has anointed me to preach good news to the poor' (Is 61:1; Lk 4:18). Hence, the use by the elders of oil in the context of prayer points beyond a purely medicinal use to an invocation of the Holy Spirit as the devine agent behind all the healing.

In any case there would be many conditions of sickness where a soothing oil would be pointless purely as a therapeutic agent. A malignant growth deep within the body is not going to be affected by the application of some oil to the patient's forehead! It is spiritual therapy that is here in view. The oil would seem simply to be an aid to the patient to think beyond the material symbol to the divine person whose activity is being symbolized.

The great problem in understanding the passage is the reference to the prayer of faith. Clearly it is crucial to the result that follows, namely, healing. Obviously healing does not always follow. Yet in the statement there is no 'maybe' or 'perhaps'. It is quite straightforward and definite: 'the prayer offered in faith will make the sick person well; the Lord will raise him up'.

In coming to an understanding of the verse it is important to clear up one issue. The sickness in view is not of necessity the consequence of specific sinfulness, whether in terms of the natural outcome of misuse of the body or on the other hand of God's chastening, as was the case of the sickness in the Corinthian church. It is possible that there may be such an explanation, but it is not necessarily so. Hence James adds: 'If he has sinned he will be forgiven.'

The fact, however, that the issue of personal sinfulness is only mentioned as a possibility should guard us from the totally false conclusion, and a very injurious one at that, that all sickness pre-supposes personal sinful failure. Job's comforters may have come to that false conclusion, and so also the Pharisees in the face of the pitiable state of the blind man (Jn 9:1 ff.). The elders of the church of Christ must not jump to that conclusion. It must be considered as a possibility, and dealt with if, in fact, it is truly a factor. It must not, however, be assumed that it is inevitably to be presumed as a cause.

One grievous misunderstanding has left many godly people perplexed and even devastated. It is when they have prayed earnestly for healing either for themselves or for a loved one and yet there has been no healing. Added to their grief can be a feeling of guilt that somehow there has been a failure in the area of faith—if only they had believed more perhaps the Lord would have healed; maybe, indeed, it is because of their own sinfulness that they did not pray the prayer of faith. It is the condition both for multiplied trouble and grief and the opportunity for Satan the accuser to continue his demoralizing activity.

In fact, all the frustration, agony and sorrow are rooted in a false view of the prayer of faith. Admittedly the reason for that false view is sometimes an erroneous teaching on the subject, suggesting that the faith that is exercised is to be stretched by personal endeavour. So the poor Christian tries hard to screw up his faith to the utmost. He confesses every known sin and sometimes searches desperately for any undetected sinful failure. He tries his best to raise his faith to a higher level. Yet all he is doing is engaging in a psychological exercise, trying frantically to persuade himself that he is confident that God will heal.

All this agonizing effort fails to see that the faith that claims a specific answer from God is itself the gift of the God who purposes to give a certain blessing, namely healing, and in his hidden ministry in our hearts moves us to pray. Paul speaks of this issue in Romans 8:26–27. He acknowledges that there are times when the Christian does not know in specific terms what he should ask for. Now clearly Paul knew in general how he should pray. He could pray with confidence for the success of the gospel, for the building up of the church, for the restoration of the backsliders, for the growth in holiness of the believers. Yet there were situations, and there still are, when it is not clear in specific and precise terms what we should pray for. Prayer for healing can be one such situation.

It is true that we can pray that God's will should be done. In the face of illness, when we are unclear we can obviously pray with great earnestness for healing, yet still with the proviso 'if it is your will'. Such praying will, of course, lead to rejoicing if the blessing sought is granted. It will also be prepared for the possibility of disappointed hopes, knowing that God sometimes has something in view that is even better than bodily health, or even continuance of life in this world.

James 5:15, however, does not envisage the possibility of healing not being granted. Rather, it states quite firmly that in response to the prayer of faith the sick one will be healed, which brings us back to the basic issue of the nature of the prayer of faith. This in turn takes us back to Romans 8. Paul does not end in uncertainty when he does not know what to pray for. He turns to the one who knows the mind and will of God, namely, the Holy Spirit. He is the indwelling Spirit in the life of the Christian. He is also the Spirit who intercedes according to the will of God. So in our ignorance and weakness we find ourselves cast upon the great Intercessor. In the deep groanings within our heart that cannot find expression in words, the Spirit is working. Our heavenly Father is the one who has sent the Spirit to us. He knows the mind of the Spirit just as the Spirit knows the will of God. In that meeting point within our hearts of the Spirit's knowledge and the Father's purpose, our poor stumbling efforts are transmuted into believing prayer.

A further help to understanding the prayer of faith is found in James' reference to Elijah (Jas 5:17). The prophet prayed for drought as a token of God's judgement and then for rain as a sign of God's mercy. The confidence of his petitions indicates that he was praying the prayer of faith. However, it must be remembered that faith is not some induced attitude; it is a divinely prompted response to the word of the Lord. Elijah had a revelation of the drought and also of the rain. This suggests that when the elders pray in faith and see the answer they are responding to God's word to them. While there is a general application of God's word to God's people, there is also the specific application to particular individuals on a special occasion. It is this indefinable, though none the less real, inward impression granted by the Spirit that draws out in response the prayer of faith.

Applying all this to an understanding of James 5:15, it seems to me that the prayer of faith is not some desperate attempt of the believer to besiege heaven. It is instead God's gracious gift to us of a specific request that is to be presented on that precise occasion. So the elders will go at the request of the sick person. The Spirit may lay a restraint upon them in that they get no further than commending the sick one to the grace of God, and to whatever God in his wisdom purposes to do. But they may be so stirred and moved by the Holy Spirit that in fact they find themselves being prompted to pray in a quite unpremeditated way for healing.

The prayer of faith is thus the Spirit's gift, one that he may bestow or withhold in accordance with his own sovereignty, and his inner knowledge of the will of God. To be restrained from praying the prayer of faith does not imply unbelief on the part of the elders. It may mean that they are walking in step with the Spirit, and so they are open to his restraint as well as to his constraint. Their silence or their qualified praying will not, therefore, reflect an evil heart of unbelief, but a godly caution begotten by the Spirit. On the other hand, their direct bold and clear request for healing will not be the product of determined effort on their part, but rather will be due to the constraint of the Spirit who moves them to pray quite specifically for healing.

Such an understanding of James' teaching imposes great responsibilities on the elders. The Spirit who thus restrains or constrains is the Holy Spirit. Those who would be instruments of his work of intercession must, therefore, be open to his direction, and must also be aiming at holiness of life, which is the context in which he works. He is also the Spirit of unity (see Eph 4:3). This means that breaches of fellowship between the elders must be guarded against and dealt with if they occur. It is as they walk in holiness of life and in loving fellowship together that they will be ready to listen to the Spirit's prompting, and be amenable to his pressure upon their hearts as they aim to pray according to the will of God.

The main thrust of this chapter—and I trust that it reflects biblical teaching—is that ultimately the Lord is the great healer. He is, however, the sovereign Lord, and all our thinking, speaking and praying must be controlled by this basic truth, that sovereignty was displayed in the Lord's earthly ministry not only in the area of granting healing but also when he withheld healing. As noted earlier the healing at Bethesda graciously singled out one needy person in the midst of a crowd. That, of necessity, meant that for his own unexplained and sovereignly determined reasons, the other sick persons were not healed. Yet on another occasion all who came were healed.

The reigning Christ in heaven is still operative in the world through his Holy Spirit. The Spirit is 'another

Counsellor', that is to say, one sent on behalf of and working in lieu of the Christ who has sent him. The power and compassion of Jesus in his earthly ministry are thus still operative in the world today. When we sing the words of the hymn; 'Your touch has still its ancient power', we are not engaged in either liturgical sentimentality or wishful thinking. We are affirming our confidence in a biblically attested fact.

That power and that compassion must, however, never be divorced from the awesome reality of his sovereignty. This means that there will be times when we are perplexed by his activity or by what seems, to unbelieving hearts, his inactivity. We may even be tempted to question his love or his pity. Yet faith comes back with a firm assertion that the Lord is King and we will gladly submit to his will even if it is painful for us. Yet his sovereignty is always gracious, always compassionate, even though through our tears we may at first find it hard to trace his grace and pity. When we say, 'He is Lord,' we are at the same time saying, 'He is love'.

Thus, while in his sovereign mercy he may grant healing, he may also permit sickness, and in either case his love will be the same. It will not do for us to argue that if we love someone deeply we would never allow them to suffer if we could prevent that suffering. We see things not only with the blurred vision of those who are still affected by indwelling sin, but also with the short-sightedness that can only focus on time and glimpses eternity with impaired clarity.

The Lord sees things not only from the standpoint of perfect holiness but from the wide perspective of eternity. Hence his concern for our character and our spiritual maturity is so great that he will permit the sickness of the body where it is conducive to that greater purpose. Similarly he will allow a terminal illness to bring what we call a premature death, because he is operating in terms of eternity. His purposes are thus being worked out in a much wider context.

A notable example of this is his dealing with Paul recorded in 2 Corinthians 12:7–10. The apostle's initial concern was for deliverance from his 'thorn in the flesh'. Being the man he was it is certain that this desire was not rooted in a desire for personal comfort, but was doubtless related to his passion to be of maximum use in the work of the kingdom. Yet the Lord's firm and repeated answer to the cry for deliverance was 'No'. Paul had to learn that there was a greater good than bodily well-being. It was a fresh and deeper realization of the wonder of God's grace that was seen in its vivid brightness against the dark background of his own unrelieved suffering.

It is no wonder, therefore, that he learned to glory in his sicknesses (he uses precisely the same word as that used in Matthew 8:17 to speak of Christ bearing our sicknesses). His glorying in this painful continuance was not due to some masochistic tendency breaking to the surface in his mind! Rather it was because of his acceptance of the Lord's assurance that in his weakness 'Christ's power' might be experienced (2 Cor 12:9).

Henry Frost quotes from the testimony of Hudson Taylor, the founder of the China Inland Mission. He testified that his greatest spiritual blessings had come to him in connection with his various sicknesses; that all of the most important advance movements that had taken place in the CIM, including its inception, had come as a direct result of some physical breakdown through which he had been called to pass. That testimony would be echoed by many others who, while gladly acknowledging the continuing reality of supernatural healing, yet with equal delight bow to the sovereign purposes of the God who 'in all things . . . works for the good of those who love him' (Rom 8:28).

9

A Helping Hand

In this publicity-conscious age, special recognition awaits those whose work is clearly and obviously in the view of many onlookers. In the current jargon, those who have a high profile, whether by achievement or by self-advertisement, will receive the plaudits. That is why those whose faces flicker regularly on the millions of TV screens are extolled as 'personalities' when in fact all they may have is a ready tongue and an equally ready wit. By contrast, those whose inventive minds have created the programme, together with the skilled cameraman and engineers who have produced it, are reduced to a list of names whose appearance is the signal to the viewer that it is time for a break to brew a cup of tea! Yet without all the supporting team, the most able presenter would have no opportunity to say anything.

During the Second World War there grew an increasing awareness of the vital importance of those whose supportive role was largely unseen, but whose tasks were vital to the achievement of the final strategy. The phrase 'back-room boys' became increasingly common, extending, as some of the bastions of male chauvinism crumbled, to include the 'back-room girls'. It has been a phrase widely applicable in the whole area of scientific, medical and technological advance of our generation. The awards for industry, the knighthoods, the Nobel prizes—these inevitably go to the front people. They, however, will pay tribute again and again to the support teams, without whom they could never have achieved the outstanding performances for which they have been honoured.

Sadly, in the church of God, worldly standards of assessment are all too often applied. Those at the front— the preachers, the missionaries, the leaders—are lauded, while the unseen workers—the praying people, the secretaries, the toilers in the obscure corners of church life— are summed up in the old saying 'out of sight, out of mind'. Yet they are the people who give both body and life to a congregation. It is their love, their patience, their giving, their working, that enable the preacher to proclaim his message in a spiritually congenial context, and that encourage the hard-pressed missionary overseas to persist in the assurance that the back-room team will not fail.

In discussion of the gifts of the Spirit, the same worldly tendency is evident, whether in the particular charismata that are the inevitable topic, or in the ignoring of those gifts that are less striking to the superficial observer. Some gifts are, by their very nature, public gifts. Preaching, evangelism and teaching are ministries that of necessity are exercised in the open. Healing, while it may happen in the privacy of the home, will inevitably be seen when the formerly sick person emerges into full health and vigour—even though Jairus' daughter was restored to life in her own home, and even though Jesus forbade publicity, the children in the neighbourhood would quickly recognize that a striking miracle had taken place. However, the fact that these gifts presuppose a public forum must not lead us to grade them in an ascending scale of importance. Every gift is important, for in every gift the Holy Spirit is accomplishing his total plan for the glorifying of Christ. All of which brings us to the obscure and often unnoticed charisma, 'helps'.

This is the only time in the Greek New Testament that this word is used. However, the closely allied verb 'to help' is employed in contexts that bring out its meaning. It was used by Luke when he recorded the song of Mary as she magnified the Lord who had 'helped his servant Israel', (Lk 1:54). It was when Israel had been given the demonstration in their own national history of spiritual and moral failure that they were in the position to receive a help that met them in their helplessness. That same thought of helping those who cannot help themselves is seen in Paul's exhortation to the elders at Ephesus, 'We must help the weak' (Acts 20:35).

The Greek prefix to the noun and the verb is the preposition *anti*, which may be translated 'in place of' or 'instead of'. So to help someone is to step right into their situation and minister to needs that they are themselves unable to meet. It is worth noticing that when Paul used the word at Ephesus he was not simply referring to his apostolic ministry or his preaching. He had just mentioned his bout of tent-making, when 'These hands of mine supplied my own needs and the needs of my companions' (Acts 20:34). Then he added the exhortation by referring to the way in which he demonstrated how this was to be done: 'I showed you that by this kind of hard work we must help the weak' (verse 35).

An initial question may well be asked: how does this gift differ from the ordinary helpfulness that is seen among non-Christians, and in the general helpfulness displayed in the life of the average congregation? By way of reply, we go back to the biblical doctrine of God. He is the Creator who has created man in his own image. Even though the image has been disastrously tarnished by human sinfulness, the evidence of our divine origin is still reflected in the frequently-shown readiness to help one another. God in his general benevolence to the human race restrains people from the full consequences of their sin, so that their consciences are still stirred by the needs of others. It is a mark of divine judgement, as Paul points out in Romans 1:18ff., when God loosens the reins of moral restraint. The result is greed, anarchy and bloodshed.

If helpfulness in the world at large is evidence of the common grace of God the Creator, then helpfulness in the church should reflect the special grace of God the Redeemer. When the Lord saves a sinner by means of the new birth, he renews the image that has been defaced by sin; and in the process of sanctification he renews that image into increasing clarity until finally in heaven the believer perfectly reflects the glory of the God who created, saved, kept and glorified him.

In the process of sanctification, the growth of the Christian in holiness of life is closely linked to growth in knowledge of God's word. As the Spirit enlightens the mind to grasp more fully the pattern of life that is God's design for the Christian, so the believer sees increasingly his or her own innate selfishness and pride. Increasingly also comes an awareness of mutual responsibility within the church as believers help one another to grow in grace. This mutual helpfulness in no way cancels concern for the community outside the church. Indeed, it is the one who is most aware of responsibility to fellow Christians who should be most aware of wider demands. Paul links the two together: 'Therefore, as we have opportunity, let us do good to all people, especially to those who belong to the family of believers' (Gal 6:10).

To summarize the main differences between the helpfulness of those who are still unbelievers and those who are now believers, the motives, the moral resources and the ultimate aims are different. The unbelievers may be kind, generous and helpful, but they are not motivated by love for God. Too often, indeed, they act either out of duty or community pressure or enlightened self-interest. Pride also will always be rearing its ugly head as it beckons the benefactor to secret self-esteem and self-congratulation. Christians, by contrast, should be moved by gratitude to the Lord who has saved them. Since God's care was extended to them and God's redeeming mercy shown even when they were rebelling against God, how dare they, how can they, withhold their love from those in need, even if they have been wronged by those who now need their help.

The resources that enable such caring also vary greatly. Non-Christians rely on the moral dynamic of their own nature. If by temperament they are genial and kind, then they will have some personal impetus. But others have a different kind of temperament, and even the genial tend to be restricted in their concerns. Christians, deeply aware as they become of their own pride and selfish ambition, know how greatly they need strength. They have come to trust in a Saviour who went around doing good (Acts 10:38), and only the Spirit of Jesus dwelling in their heart will enable them not only to persist in good works, but to extend their range to those who lie outside the circle of their own racial, social or educational prejudice.

The goals towards which the non-Christian and the Christian aim are also widely divergent. The unbeliever sees someone in great physical or material need and in compassion tries to help. What is in view is the alleviation of hunger or pain or deprivation of whatever kind it may be. That, however, is the ultimate aim. But the Christian, while also being stirred by the sufferer, and moved to try and help or heal, has further areas in view. Taught by Jesus' parable of the good Samaritan, there is a desire to help the sufferer. However, as well as the poverty or pain, there are spiritual needs to be met. Feeding the hungry stomach with bread is allied to providing the bread of life for the soul. Healing the sick bodies of the leprosy patient or the famine victim has a further goal to be reached, namely, the spiritual renewal of the sinner. In all this the supreme aim will be a powerful factor as the Christian aims to glorify God by displaying the loving concern and compassion of the Lord Jesus.

In view of all this, can we maintain that there is such a special charisma as helpfulness? The simple answer from 1 Corinthians 12:28 is 'Yes'. The particular word that Paul uses indicates that it is a similar helpfulness to that which ought to characterize Christians at large. It is a ministry extended to those who, at their particular point of need, are not able to help themselves. It is a reflection of the grace of God and the compassion of Jesus. It aims at 'the common good' of the fellowship of believers. Yet is has such a distinctiveness that it is listed as one of the charismata, graciously and with sovereign choice given by the Holy Spirit. What then is this distinctiveness?

It may help in answering this question to go back to the discussion in an earlier chapter of the gift of faith. There it was emphasized that there is no difference in essential character between the faith of the youngest Christian and the faith of Hudson Taylor or George Müller. The difference is one of degree and extent. There was an intensity, a strength, a persistence and a breadth of scope in the faith of those men that marked them out as especially gifted. So in the area of helpfulness, it is not by contrast with the attitude of other Christians, but often in the context of a deeply caring congregation that the especially gifted helper excels.

While God gives to every believer a measure of Christ's compassion, there are some in whom he works in an especial way so that they not only bring help and comfort to a wide circle of needy people, but act as a stimulus to other Christians to enlarge their own horizons and to deepen their own caring ministry. In that stimulating activity they wholly reverse the normal assessment of the value of gifts. Theirs is a behind-the-scenes ministry, and yet they can effect as great a blessing in many lives—and perhaps even greater—than that resulting from the exercise of the more public gifts.

One mark of the truly gifted person is humility. The Christian who wants to display imagined gifts is both deluded and sinful. The true exemplar of charismatic experience should be, indeed must be, humble; they could not be anything else in view of the very word that is applied. A gift is not earned. It is a not a reward for achievement or merit. It is a freely-bestowed favour given to the wholly undeserving. It is noticeable that those who are especially gifted in the area of helpfulness are often very humble in their own estimation of themselves. Indeed, in some cases their quiet ministry is such that they are almost unaware of how helpful they are. To speak to them of the charisma of helpfulness is assuredly not to encourage pride. It is simply to make them more explicitly aware of the source of their ministry, and so to prompt an even deeper humility and a glad appreciation of God's grace.

One mark of this helpfulness is its spontaneity. The world at large has to be jarred into an awareness of clamant human needs. It took the shocking pictures from Ethiopia to shake an affluent society into some degree of sensitivity to the famine-stricken and famished millions. Even in the church there often has to be an awakening challenge to rouse Christians from their comfortable and ingrown concerns. The response can, however, remain at the level of duty. But those who are really into the ministry of helping others have a spontaneous overflow of compassion that seems to keep them on the alert for any sign of need.

True helpfulness is rooted in sympathy. The helper enters imaginatively into the needs of others, and suffers in spirit with them. Such a sensitive realization of another's needs guards against certain dangers that are constantly near at hand in the caring ministry. In the first place, there is the danger of the patronizing approach. It was exemplified in the work of some, though certainly not all, middle-class ladies in the last century. Venturing out from their comfortable homes they went 'slumming' in London's East End. They brought much material help, but in many cases, while it filled empty stomachs or replaced rags with decent clothes, it left the beneficiaries deprived. They felt that they were being almost dehumanized by the condescension shown to them.

True helpfulness, however, does not depreciate another's position or lessen their self-respect. Rather, it enhances them. The true helper does not make the recipients of help feel small and diminished. Instead, the recipients are enriched with a sense of wonder and gratitude that someone else cares. Often, indeed, it points the one who is helped to Jesus himself, whether in saving faith or in grateful realization of the privilege of being a member of the body of Christ.

The gift of helpfulness also guards the possessor against the peril of weakening rather than strengthening the recipient. At the physical level, anyone who has had physiotherapy in hospital will know the blend of support and demand coming from the trained practitioner. The patient trying to coax weary or damaged limbs back into action may at times feel like protesting against the therapy. Yet at the same time there is a realization that the physiotherapist is at one and the same time giving support where it is really needed, and yet compelling the patient to develop, albeit painfully, the wasted muscles or injured joints.

The same is true in ministering to the needs of others

in a wider area. To be excessively supportive may appear to be helpful whereas, in fact, it inhibits a real renewal of the other person. Clearly, when someone has just suffered the trauma of bereavement or a bad accident or the loss of a job they will need, at the initial stage, a great deal of support. However, the true helper will have an eye to the future. The last thing one wants to see is an undue dependence on those who give support. Such dependence, coupled with self-pity, can delay the process of mental and emotional healing. The helper who is both loving and wise will know when whole-hearted undergirding is needed, and when a gentle pressure towards a renewed confidence may require a lessening of this very full support. There will obviously be an on-going ministry of helpfulness but, like the therapy in hospital, it will aim at renewal, in this case of emotional, mental and, above all, spiritual resources.

A truly sensitive spirit will also guard against forcing help upon someone who either does not need it or does not wish to receive it. I recall the amusing story of two Boy Scouts who in an excess of zeal to do their daily good turn, brushed aside the protests of the old lady and helped her to cross the busy road. The trouble was, she did not actually want to cross the road and her protests were not an assertion of her own ability to get across, but simply a statement that she was already on the right side! The spiritually-anointed helper will neither intrude into another's privacy, nor brusquely sweep aside another's expressed wishes. Rather, there will be a gentleness of touch that is the hallmark of a truly sensitive ministry to others.

A further characteristic of this ministry is its quiet persistence. The compassion of the world at large is notoriously short-lived. It is stirred into action by a crisis, whether at a local level by a sudden death or crippling accident, or at a national or international level by some massive disaster. Ask the survivors of some past earth-quake how they have fared since the crisis and they will often speak of a wonderful initial assistance that soon ebbed to leave them struggling with their devastated lives. In the individual realm the same is true. A funeral elicits a great wave of sympathy, which sadly ebbs to make the long-term loneliness even more stark. The true helper is not an occasional sympathizer, but a continuing support.

The gift of helpfulness seems to be closely allied with spiritual discernment. Those whom God blesses with this gift seem to have a sharp awareness of areas of need, and also of the kind of consequence that will follow. This means a sensitive recognition of the danger signs in someone whose distress has not yet reached such a pitch that it inevitably becomes apparent to many. It is like a radar that picks up an incoming aeroplane long before the craft comes within sight. The helper seems to have sensitive spiritual antennae that pick up the warning signal of the troubled or needy person. They will detect a look in the eyes, or sense the tone of voice, or read between the lines of a letter, and will realize, sometimes long before the general run of people are aware of it, that something is wrong. Indeed, they may be able to act with understanding and concern at the very early stages with such effect that the incipient threat does not materialize, simply because the need has been already met.

Such discernment will also look ahead and read the map of likely developments. It does not need prophetic insight to know that the person in trouble will have particular occasions ahead that may add to the pain. There will be a birthday, a wedding anniversary, or Christmas, all of which may deepen the agonizing memory of happier days. Similarly, there is a realization that normal developments will bring further crises. The young widow with small children will, in due course, be facing the problem of teenagers with no partner to assist.

The sufferer from some wasting disease will know that the outlook is bleak and anticipation will easily cast a shadow even over present joys. The true helper will be aware of these and many other areas of need, and will be alert to bring support.

This gift, like many others, will develop by use. One who has had long experience of ministering to people in need will acquire a great deal of knowledge about the varieties of human temperament. They may not become versed in technical psychological distinction between introverts and extroverts. They may not be able to list the temperamental differences between phlegmatic, choleric, melancholic, etc. Yet they will recognize that one person will react in a very different way from someone else, even though the situation of stress may be almost identical. The Spirit-led helper will not engage in the facile exercise of handing out ready-made solutions. Rather, there will be an attempt to give advice or practical help that is tailored to the special requirements of the individual. This kind of personal ministry will take into account the temperament, the spiritual maturity or immaturity and the actual situation of that very special individual.

Many readers may feel, indeed they ought to feel, that all this should characterize every Christian. All of us should aim to develop such a caring concern for others. A congregation that is truly alive spiritually should exemplify this compassionate attitude. God, however, in his wisdom knows that, while this should be the case, the endemic selfishness of indwelling sin constantly turns our thought to ourselves. So, while reminding us constantly from the Scriptures that we should bear one another's burdens, he also equips some of his people in a special way. His aim is not that they should carry the neglected burdens that others have failed to carry. Their gift is not intended to be a substitute for others' neglect. Nor is it intended to release others from the obligation of love for others. Rather, he intends it to stir us all, whether by shaming the self-centred, stirring the lethargic, or stimulating to increased activity those who are already engaged in ministering to others in need.

If there is one kind of person who might qualify for the title of the unconscious charismatic, it is the one with this gift. To point out to them that it is one of the charismata is not with a view to inflating their ego or making them self-conscious in their ministry. It is simply to give them a deep sense of wonder that God should have been so gracious as to give them this very precious gift. It should also keep them from becoming irritated or annoyed when they see other Christians who are seemingly unconcerned. They will realize that if they themselves are deeply concerned, it is not because of some innate personal superiority but by the grace of God alone. In times of discouragement also, they will be heartened, especially when their helpfulness may have been rewarded with ingratitude. They will remember that the God of grace who gave his Son to die has so often seen those redeemed by the blood of the cross sadly ungrateful for all that they have received. So, with a renewed realization that their own caring ministry is itself a reflection of the grace of their Saviour, they can forget the plaudits and reject the inner desire to have a more public role. To be a helper is to tread in the steps of one who, before he went to Calvary, was content to do the menial work of a slave and wash his disciples' feet.

10

Miracles

I have a newspaper cutting on my desk as I write. It was
an advertisement for a meeting which, naturally enough,
was designed to catch people's attention in order to
persuade them to attend. The bold print at the top asks a
question: 'Need a Miracle?' The subsidiary question asks:
'What miracle do you need: "Marriage? Finance? Healing
of Body?" Jesus is the Answer.' Then follows the invitation to come to the meeting at which these hoped-for
miracles were presumably expected to happen. Under-
neath the advertisement was a newspaper reference,
probably quite without malice but perhaps indicating the
understanding of a typical sub-editor. It read: 'More
entertainments appear on pages 4 & 5'.

Some Christians reading the advert would probably
have shuddered or reflected that this kind of approach
has sadly long been abroad in Christian circles, where the
invitation to a meeting has been set in the framework of
displaying some of the benefits of the gospel. We are
probably familiar with the approach: 'Do you want joy,
purpose, direction, etc? Then come to Jesus.' I remember
my eardrums being assaulted by a loudspeaker on a
passing car or van blaring out a similar item: 'If you want

joy, real joy, wonderful joy, let Jesus come into your heart!'

Other Christians with a much more penetrating criticism would not simply dismiss this kind of approach, but would comment that it confirms all their fears and suspicions of all things charismatic. Are miracles, they may query, there for the asking? Can the power to work miracles be guaranteed for a certain time on a Saturday afternoon? One can sympathize with their reactions without, however, accepting that to maintain the continuance of the gift of working miracles, as promised in 1 Corinthians 12:10,28, commits one either to the crudity of the advert or to the more serious position of laying claims quite so easily to miraculous powers.

Incidentally, there was an alleged miracle of healing that day with someone throwing away the sticks that had been an aid to a badly crippled condition. In fact I knew the person well and, tragically, months later she was still by and large in the same condition of serious physical disability as she had been for years past. However, to many who were there and did not know the outcome, it seemed to be a miracle—a young person told me a year or so later that he had been impressed that day by the wonder. But then he did not know the tragedy of continuing serious physical handicap. Such knowledge can lead to a cynical dismissal of the whole issue and we can sympathize with those who feel like that. However, the old saying about throwing out the baby with the bathwater applies here. We are to be governed not by extravagant claims, nor by spurious results, but by the teaching of Scripture.

From the standpoint of the teaching of 1 Corinthians 12, both those who make wild claims and those who reject totally the expectation of miracles are alike in violation of the basic principle of that chapter, which is the sovereignty of the Spirit of God. Thus Paul emphasizes that the Spirit gives gifts as he wills. He it is who chooses when to give, when not to give, upon whom to bestow the gifts, and from whom to withhold them. So it is invalid for one group to argue that because God graciously gives some gifts he must of necessity be required by bold asking to give all. Likewise it is absurd for the critic to insist that those who accept the continuance of the charismata must produce evidence of miracles or else abstain from every claim, saying that if one charisma is not being exercised then no gifts are to be claimed. Both sides need to read again Paul's questions in verses 29 and 30, to which the implied answer is 'No'.

Turning to the actual words employed by the New Testament, we discover different facets of the meaning of the term 'miracle'. There is the Greek word *teras,* which means 'wonder'. Obviously it reflects the kind of impact that miracles made on people. Those who witnessed the extraordinary deeds of Jesus were astonished. They recognized actions that were of such a supernatural character that people were filled with awe. It is significant, however, as Origen (one of the theologians of the early centuries) pointed out, that the word 'wonder' is never used by itself to describe a miracle in the New Testament. It is coupled with another word, in a phrase such as 'signs and wonders'.

This usage reflects the attitude of Jesus, for whom the extraordinary nature of his miracles was secondary. He did not come to be a wonder-worker but a Saviour. He had no interest in the emotional stirring produced by his miracles, and indeed rebuked those whose excitement reflected not a spiritual response but a feverish curiosity. While the miracles certainly are wonders, that is not their primary significance.

Another word employed is *dunamis*, which means 'power'. It is reflected in our English words 'dynamic' or 'dynamite'. It focuses our attention on the enormous energy that, as it were, bursts into action. It is not an increase of natural power that is in view. It is the dynamic that lies behind the creation of the universe and sustains its vast complexity, which, in the miracles of Jesus, erupts into the normal pattern of living. Thus in a fierce storm the latent power of creation is let loose, but when the raging winds on the lake meet the power of Jesus they are stilled by an even greater demonstration of the same power that whipped them up in the first place.

The third word is *semeion*, which means 'sign'. It is a key word in John's Gospel, whose selection of miracles is presented as a cumulative testimony to Jesus as the Son of God. Each wonderful work is also a sign pointing beyond the display of power. It is intended to force questions from the onlookers. Who is this person who does such deeds? Whence comes this marvellous power? Indeed, it was precisely such a question that was wrung from those who witnessed the stilling of the storm 'What kind of man is this? Even the winds and the waves obey him!' (Mt 8:27). John gives the answer to such questions and summarizes his aim in recording the seven signs: 'But these are written that you may believe that Jesus is the Christ, the Son of God, and that by believing you may have life in his name' (Jn 20:31).

John also uses another word as he speaks of the miracles simply as works (*erga*). Trench, in his book on the miracles, put it so well: 'They are simply "works" as though the wonderful were only the natural form of working for him who is dwelt in by all the fulness of God . . . The great miracle is the Incarnation; all else, so to speak, follows naturally and of course. It is no wonder that he whose name is Wonderful (Isaiah 9:6) does works of wonder; the only wonder would be if he did them not.'[9]

A further comment is necessary: the miracles of Scripture are not confined to healings. That comment is even more needed today in view of the tendency to support claims to miraculous happenings by pointing to remarkable healings that have the authentic mark of direct divine intervention. That is in no way to minimize the miraculous character of such extraordinary healings. It is simply to underline the fact that the two actions—healings and displays of miraculous power—are not synonymous.

This distinction is brought out clearly in the list of gifts that Paul gives in 1 Corinthians 12. He speaks quite specifically of 'gifts of healings'. The charisma of miracle-working power is, however, a distinct gift. If, then, there are claims to the latter power, we would expect to see them verified by works other than instances of direct divine healing, supernatural and wonderful as these undoubtedly are. If a list of the miracles of Jesus is examined it will be noticed that a little more than half of them are healings. Then there are the allied areas of casting out demons and raising from the dead. That still leaves nearly a quarter of his miracles in a different category, whether in miraculous provision—like the feeding of the crowds or the draughts of fishes—or in demonstrations of power over the forces of nature.

Before moving to the crucial issue as to whether there is any evidence for the continuance of such miracles after the period of biblical revelation, or indeed whether the Bible gives any ground for expecting such happenings, it will be important to look more closely at what is meant by a miracle. This is especially important in view of the kind of humanist derision that implies that Christians believe in a topsy-turvy world in which the deity rather capriciously decides every now and then to take a hand in the proceedings. By contrast with this gross caricature, the humanist points to his eminently rational view of the world. In that ordered system one can see the clear evidence of cause and effect following in logical sequence. The so-called laws of nature are thus descriptive formulae to underline this cause-and-effect sequence. Thus the law of gravity does not make the apple fall. It simply affirms that every time an object that is heavier than air is released it will fall to the ground.

By way of reply to the scornful objector to miracles, it may be useful to begin where he and we both are, namely, in the realm of everyday experience. We go to Heathrow Airport and a jumbo jet, which is vastly heavier than an apple, is heaving not only its own bulk but a huge load of passengers and cargo into the air. We have no problems in explaining that there is no violation of the law of gravity. It is simply that, just as an outstretched hand stops the apple's fall, so the thrust of the engines more than cancels the gravitational pull on the aircraft. In short, there is the intervention of a third factor, which itself fits into a pattern of orderly existence.

In a similar way, the totally unexpected direction that events take in a miracle are not due to a violation of the natural order. After all, what we call the natural order is really the Creator's order. The cause-and-effect sequence is the pattern that God has built into the structure of physical existence. However, the Creator may, for his own good purposes, intervene in the orderly scheme and interpose a further factor. A water-skier skims on the surface because of the pull of the speedboat and the supporting skis, so that the natural tendency to sink is counteracted. In the case of Jesus walking on the water there was no physical support, but the Creator who sustains the whole universe in space was easily able to interpose the divinely-given buoyancy so that both Jesus and Peter walked on the water. The normal pattern, however, was still in being so that the moment the divine intervention was withdrawn Peter began to sink (Mt 14:22–33).

The miraculous intervention does not, therefore, plunge the world into a chaos of random happenings and arbitrary actions by the whim of an erractic being. Rather, when God works a miracle, he fits the unusual event into the ongoing scheme. Thus, as C. S. Lewis in his brilliant book *Miracles* pointed out, when God miraculously created a unique spermatozoon in the womb of Mary, the normal processes of implantation and pregnancy proceeded. Similarly, when the thousands were miraculously fed they then had to chew and digest the bread so amazingly provided.

Another factor needs to be noted. Sometimes, in working a miracle God uses a natural process but controls the time factor in a supernatural way. Thus, in the ordinary course of annual growth the sun and rain and minerals from the soil are used by the God who gives the harvest in order to produce the grapes. At Cana, however, the Lord as it were telescoped the whole process of fermentation, so that in a moment God short-circuited the natural process which he uses every season to turn water into wine (again, see Lewis on *Miracles*). In both cases the end result was wine but at Cana the great husbandman dispensed with all the intervening steps.

There is another type of event in which we see the miraculous element in God's use of time. We are familiar with the biblical teaching on providence by which God interlocks events to produce a desired result. The man of the world may speak of chance, or good fortune, or the luck of the draw. The Christian, however, recognizes the overruling providence of God and constantly rejoices in the details of daily living that display God's providential care. Yet there are occasions when the timing of two events is so remotely improbable in terms of mathematical probability that the coinciding of the two happenings can only be ascribed to divine timing to a marvellous degree. The crossing of the Jordan by Israel was such an occurrence. The biblical record tells of the damming of the waters much further upstream, probably by the collapse of the banks. This occurrence has happened since that time and has been recorded. What, however, made that particular damming of the river so extraordinary as to be described as miraculous was that it happened at precisely the time when the priests were leading the people down into a river swollen by flood water. In a day when there was no radio link between the two points on the Jordan, the precise timing was so extraordinary that one has to presuppose a supernatural control of events.

One final element in the miracles of Scripture is of especial significance in a day when those who rather lightly claim or advertise miracles seem to assume that such miracles will be beneficial and thrilling to those who experience their powerful impact. In the Bible, however, this is not always so. The Old Testament had its miracles of judgement as in the infliction of leprosy on Elisha's servant (2 Kings 5:20–27), the solemn judgement by pestilence on David's pride (2 Sam 24:11–15), or the warning handwriting on the wall of the Babylonian palace (Dan 5:5). In the miracles of Jesus there is only one miracle of judgement and it was on a barren fig tree. Yet, in fact, it was a particularly awesome sign in that it spoke of the coming judgement upon Israel.

After Pentecost there were miraculous signs but not all of them were directly beneficial. True there is the opening of the prison doors for Peter (Acts 12:6–10), the delivering earthquake at Philippi (Acts 16:25–26) and the raising from the dead of Dorcas (Acts 9:40–41) and Eutychus (Acts 20:9–12). But there are also the awe-inspiring miracles of judgement as Ananias and Sapphira are suddenly smitten down (Acts 5:1–10); there are the judgemental sickness and deaths in Corinth (1 Cor 11:30); and there is the blinding of Elymas in Cyprus (Acts 13:11). This kind of miracle would hardly fit into the kind of expectation encouraged by the advertisement in my newspaper cutting!

We may seem to have been a long time in reaching the central question of this chapter, namely, whether miracles may be expected to occur today. It has, however, been important to deal at such length with the nature of biblical miracles since so much superficial thinking and so many spurious claims emerge from a basic failure to be clear about what we really mean when we speak about miracles. To summarize, we are referring to extraordinary interventions into the normal sequence of events. Those demonstrations of divine power that elicit awe and wonder in those who see them are signs pointing beyond themselves to the God who stands behind them. They are never, in Scripture, scattered freely in the ongoing history of God's people. They appear often at high points of divine revelation, and while sometimes they speak of mercy, and sometimes of judgement, they always speak of God. The Creator intervenes whether by interposing a new and powerful factor, or by telescoping the natural processes of the physical world, or by a supernatural ordering of the timing of events.

Since miracles have this aim of bearing witness to the Saviour, they are never intended either to satisfy the inquisitive or to stir the emotionally excitable. Rather, they should produce reverence and godly fear. They are subordinate to the word of God. For Jesus, his word was his supreme testimony; his works were auxiliaries to reinforce his words. To those, therefore, who were simply looking for phenomena, he either rebuked them or removed himself from them. Matthew twice records him (12:39; 16:4) giving a stern reply to the shallow unbelievers: 'A wicked and adulterous generation asks for a miraculous sign! But none will be given it except the sign of the prophet Jonah.' That sign of Jonah pointed to Jesus' burial and to his resurrection on the third day. The same rebuke is implicit in the parable of the rich man and the poor man. If the brothers of the rich man would not heed the Scriptures, then they would not be persuaded even though someone rose from the dead (Luke 16:31).

Speaking personally, I find great difficulty in understanding the full import of a key statement of Jesus. It was uttered in one of the final discourses before he went to his trial and death. It was specifically directed not to the apostles but to 'anyone who has faith in me' (Jn 14:12). That is a most important reference in the debate as to whether the apostles alone were to be the agents of miraculous activity. Jesus certainly clearly seems to be looking far beyond them to the general circle of believers.

What then is promised to any believer? It is that 'he who believes in me will also do the works that I do, and greater works than these will he do, because I go to the Father' (Revised Standard Version). The latter part of that statement may at first sight seem to be the difficult one. However, in my judgement, it is more easily understood. If Jesus was speaking here of miracles of healing or cursing, of natural provision or of controlling nature, then there is no evidence in the New Testament that the apostles did greater works.

What greater works could there be than feeding five thousand unless it were to feed fifty thousand? What greater power could be displayed than stilling a storm unless it were to still a whole series of tempests? It seems evident that Jesus was referring to a totally different kind of miracle. If we reflect on the fact that the spiritual rebirth of the Christian is likened to a resurrection (Eph 2:5) or to a new creation (2 Cor 5:17), then it seems very clear that the greater works are the widespread harvesting of souls in which the thousands of converts after Pentecost were firstfruits.

It is, however, the first part of his statement that is so challenging to the expositor. When he speaks to his own contemporaries of 'the works that I do' he is speaking surely of the miracles that he had been working. As we

138

saw earlier, John often uses the word 'works' as another term for 'miracles', as if the wonderful one could only be expected to do wonderful works. This means that Jesus is speaking of the kind of miracles described in the Gospels. But he is referring to future days and to the general run of believers. They, then, will do similar works. They will perform similar miracles.

Paul's reference in 1 Corinthians 12 is to the charisma given by the risen Lord through the Holy Spirit. That gift is the ability to work miracles. He uses two words in the phrase translated in the Revised Standard Version 'the working of miracles'. The second word is one of those discussed earlier, namely *dunamis*, which means 'power'. In the plural, as it is here, it refers to powerful deeds. The word that is translated 'working' is the same as that used in verse 6. These two verses are the only occasions in the Greek New Testament where the word is used. Its meaning suggests the doing of something by putting in effort. It has a close affinity with our English word 'energy' (Greek, *energema*). So one might well translate it as 'activities that produce miracles'. The reference is, therefore, not to the miracle that God does directly and in which the one who benefits is passive, as were Paul and Barnabas in the prison at Philippi. It speaks rather of one who is actively involved, whether by word or action, as Peter was when Ananias and Sapphira were suddenly stricken.

Have, then, such miracles been wrought since the days of the apostles? Indeed, should we even envisage the possibility of their being performed today? The answer from one quarter will be a triumphant challenge: 'Show me your miracles!' Where and by whom are they being wrought? The answer from the other side is either to point to remarkable healings or to make claims that do not always stand up to scrutiny. I believe that neither of these reactions is the primary response.

We must begin with the biblical teaching and then see how we view our present situation—and by the latter I do not mean the situation in Britain but the condition of things in the world-wide church. As far as the biblical position is concerned, I have tried to argue in chapter 2 of this book that the biblical evidence points to a continuance of the charismata beyond the apostolic age. One cannot then detach one or more of these gifts from that general position. The claim for their continuance means that either all continue or none continue. I maintain, therefore, that the general biblical thesis that the gifts continue applies to all the gifts.

Earlier in this present chapter it was noted that Jesus in John 14 was clearly speaking about the future continuance of miraculous powers. However, he did not limit their performance to the apostles to whom he was speaking, for this would have rooted such powers decisively in the first century. Rather, he widened the circle of application to 'anyone who has faith in me'. That category cannot possibly be restricted to the apostolic era. Since it is a basic description of any Christian, it would seem to have a continuing application until the second coming of Christ when faith shall give way to immediate sight of the Lord. The underlying principle of divine sovereignty, of course, always applies in the distribution of all of God's gifts. However, that sovereign bestowal is not for one group of believers in the first century, but for any believer in any age on whom the Holy Spirit, in his sovereign freedom, bestows the gift.

Strangely, some of those who insist on present evidence adopt a different stance when talking about revival. They believe, rightly in my judgement, that there are times when God visits his people with quite extraordinary power and when, as a result, whole communities or even whole nations are deeply affected. Push them to show an English awakening in their lifetime and they will naturally say that there has not been such. Indeed, they must admit that the last awakening on such a major national scale was two centuries ago. They will, however, be quick to add that other lands have had similar visitations in this century. They are perfectly justified in coupling their admission of absence of revival in England with a strong reference to evidence from overseas of which they have no direct personal experience, since they believe that the reports stand up to examination. They still vigorously insist that examination of the Acts indicates a quality of spiritual life and a power in witness and preaching that have been seen again and again, though not in their own experience.

I ask such to apply this response to the area of charismatic gifts in general, and to this issue of the working of miracles in particular. Let them concede that the very arguments that they use to urge prayer for revival have a wider application. So those who may admit that they have not seen in their limited personal experience the kind of miracle seen in the Acts may yet argue—primarily from the teaching of Scripture, but then secondarily from history, and from reports from other lands—that to claim the continuance of miracles is neither to join the ranks of the charlatans nor to endorse the dubious allegations of the miraculous in which Roman Catholicism specializes!

Earlier it was noted that the miracles in the Bible clustered around high points of revelation when God by mighty deeds made himself known. This is true in the Old Testament. Thus at the time of the Exodus, and again during the conflict between Elijah and Elisha and the prophets of Baal, miracles are much in evidence. It is the same in the New Testament, which is the final revelation. Thus, the coming of the Messiah, culminating in his resurrection and ascension, is a period rich in miracle. The early years of widespread gospel advance also had the attestation of miraculous signs. Yet even then, there is no pattern of miracles on demand. The storm that threatened to take the lives of Paul and others was not miraculously stilled, and it was by the very natural means of swimming and clinging to pieces of wreckage that they reached the shore.

It would seem, therefore, that an abundance of miracles is hardly to be expected in a situation where the gospel has long been preached, the churches long established and the moral consequences in the nation at large are very evident. However, in places where false religions are centuries old and where Satan and demonic agency have for generations been a dark reality, it should not surprise us if there are extraordinary manifestations of divine power that authenticate the testimony of the gospel. It is in some of these situations that the prophecy of Jesus in John 14:12 may well be fulfilled.

One problem is that such is the human tendency to exaggerate and such the credulity of some Christians that sensational reports are given. Then, when many of the alleged miracles are exposed as spurious, it is not surprising if some Christians lump all such claims together and dismiss them completely. An illustration of this is the record of the spiritual awakening in Indonesia in the 1960s. Stories circulated of an abundance of miracles, with multiplied food and walking on water, etc. A sober appraisal was given by the Overseas Missionary Fellowship. Another similar one came from Dr Stanley Moynihan of World Vision. However, while rejecting many of the exaggerated reports, he still insisted that there was evidence of the genuine. Admittedly this was largely confined to one area, the island of Timor, and to one brief period, 1965–66. Yet he still maintained that there were genuine miracles, that is, extraordinary works of power capable of being known via the senses but totally beyond human explanation.

He also pointed out that in the old days the witch

doctors had performed miracles in connection with their fetishes—doubtless it was the same demonic agency that enabled the magicians of ancient Egypt to imitate the miracles of Moses. It was not therefore surprising, he maintained, that when the gospel led people to burn these idolatrous objects that God should accompany the destruction of these fetishes by special displays of his power.

There is another kind of miracle noted earlier. It is when God in a supernatural way dovetails two events so that their precise coincidence is such an amazing display of divine providence that it can only be accounted for on the grounds of direct divine intervention. One such occurrence of this supernatural timing is recorded in the life of George Müller. He was crossing the Atlantic and had a meeting fixed for Quebec on a Saturday; but it was now Wednesday and they were at a standstill in a thick blanket of fog off Newfoundland. The captain had to meet Müller's query with an admission that it was impossible to get there in time. Müller, however, insisted that he had not missed an engagement in fifty-seven years. He suggested prayer.

Müller prayed the simplest prayer the captain had ever heard: 'O Lord, if thou wilt, remove this fog in five minutes. Thou dost know the engagement made for me in Quebec for Saturday.' He restrained the captain from praying after his own brief petition, 'First,' he said, 'because you don't believe God will do it and second, I believe he has done it so there's no need for you to pray. Open the door, Captain, and you'll find the fog gone.' And so it was. Müller kept his Saturday engagement in Quebec.[10] To those who may raise questioning or even cynical eyebrows, it needs saying that in the remarkable provision of food for hundreds of children, Müller had other demonstrations of miraculous providence when, faced with empty plates on the tables and an empty larder, sudden, last minute and quite extraordinary provision was made.

Let me add a story that I know to be utterly authentic as I know personally the godly retired minister who told it to me. It happened in the early sixties in a Leicestershire village and involved a young couple, one converted in the Christian Union at Leicester University, and the other during an RAF posting to Iraq. Being young in the faith, they had a childlike trust that more sophisticated believers sometimes tend to lose. They were getting ready for their wedding and were deeply concerned to have their unconverted relatives there to hear the gospel. The girl's father and brothers, however, were all bookmakers and Saturday was a busy day that they could not miss. There was only one hope and that was if frost closed down all racing not only in England but across the Irish Sea. Furthermore it had to be frost on Friday to ensure that bookies would not be waiting on Saturday for news. So the couple came and asked the church to pray for frost.

'Naive!' say some, 'Credulous!' say others. But this small church was largely composed of recent converts who had not learned to keep qualifying God's promises, and simply prayed for frost. The minister, who at that time was still a part-time pastor, drove to his office, and as he went towards the city the prospect for frost seemed remote. It was a sunny morning and warm for December. Frost might come in the evening but hardly during a sunny and rather warm morning. As he sat in his office he glanced out of the window at mid-morning and frost was beginning to appear on the trees. As he drove home Charnwood Forest was glistening white. Back home the news bulletin was being broadcast with an announcement of a sudden frost that affected the whole country and also, as he distinctly recalled, Northern Ireland. Racing was completely shut down.

The family of bookmakers were at the wedding

hearing the gospel and asking serious spiritual questions. One brother was not there. He was also unconverted, yet he rebuked the Christians for praying about the racing and forgetting about the football pools. He was responsible for that side of their bookmaking business! He, however, knew all about the praying, and after emigrating to Australia was converted and became a preacher. Is this a fanciful story? Well, the man whom I know and trust completely told it to me shortly before I wrote this section of the book, and he was the preacher at the wedding! I suspect that George Müller would not have been unduly surprised.

Let me end this chapter with a quotation from one of the outstanding reformed commentators of this century, the late William Hendriksen. In his commentary on John 14:12–14 he wrote: 'The disciples need not fear that Christ's physical absence will mean a loss of power to perform miracles. From heaven Jesus will continue to supply them with this power. A glorious promise is here given to the one who keeps on believing in him. Such a person will do the works which Jesus is doing . . . not only miracles in the physical realm but even greater works than these, namely miracles in the spiritual realm . . . In the book of Acts miracles are again and again linked with prayer . . . such a prayer in Christ's name will always and most certainly be answered.'[11]

11

Apostles Today

I have no difficulty in subscribing to the historic evangelical assessment of the position of the twelve apostles and also of Paul. They have a uniqueness that is reiterated throughout the New Testament. They are 'foundational' in the sense that other apostles mentioned in the New Testament are not.

What makes me so persuaded of this unique status? First of all there is the nature of their call and also their qualifications for the apostolic office and ministry. In the case of the Twelve, they were called by Jesus during his earthly ministry and had the unique dual qualification of being his companions from the days of his baptism by John, and of being eye witnesses of his resurrection.

These two qualifications were recognized by the eleven who were left after the treacherous defection of Judas Iscariot. Their replacement of the traitor by Matthias was on the basis that he had these qualifications and also that he was the appointee of the Lord whose will they sought in prayer before the final appointment took place.

It is significant that throughout the New Testament they are specially designated either as 'the twelve apostles' or more briefly as 'the Twelve'. It is clear that they had this special status in the eyes of the early believers. That this judgement was also the divine assessment is seen in the vision that the Lord gave to John on the island of Patmos, wherein the heavenly city had as its twelve foundations the twelve apostles of the Lamb (Rev 21:14).

Now this has led to mistaken notions at opposite ends of the debate. There has been the suggestion that the eleven acted precipitately as recorded in Acts 1, and that the Lord intended Paul to be the replacement for Judas. For this suggestion there is not a scrap of New Testament evidence. It ignores the period of forty days during which they had received much detailed teaching from the Lord that is not recorded. It fails also to see the implications of the fact that Luke, writing under the direct inspiration of the Holy Spirit, records the choice of Matthias but with not the slightest hint of any censure. This is all the more notable in that Luke, the companion of Paul, pens the Acts and gives a far greater prominence to Paul than he does, for example, to Peter. So Luke saw nothing incompatible in his acceptance of Paul's apostolic role and the fact that he was not one of the Twelve.

The mistake at the other end of the debate has been as that made in *Restoration* magazine, which puts Paul in a different category from the Twelve, and in the same bracket as other apostles mentioned in the New Testament such as Barnabas and James, the Lord's brother. At first sight they might appear to have warrant for such a contention. After all, is Paul not bracketed with Barnabas in Acts 14:14, where they are both together described as 'the apostles'? And again, is there not the vision in Revelation 21:14 of the twelve foundations of the city?

What they fail to see is that while Paul shared with Barnabas an apostolic ministry as a 'sent man' commissioned to blaze a pioneer missionary trail, he had other qualifications that made him quite distinct from Barnabas or James, and put him in the same bracket as the Twelve.

In the first place, and this is surely a major fact, he was directly appointed by the risen Lord. Later he was to write his letter to the Ephesians in which the ministry gifts— apostles, prophets, evangelists, pastors, teachers—are the gifts of the ascended Lord. The Lord after his ascension poured out his Spirit at Pentecost, and so the gifts described in Ephesians 4 are the gifts bestowed by the Spirit who comes now that Jesus has been glorified (Jn 7:39).

Paul's commission, however, is different. It was in a quite special sense that the risen Lord in an earthly setting set him apart. Later, in 2 Corinthians 12:1–5, Paul describes his rapture into heaven, with his visions of inexpressible wonder. But on the Damascus road it was so evidently the risen Lord himself that in no sense could it be called a vision. In fact it was as literal an appearance as those in the upper room or by the lake side. Thus in 1 Corinthians 15:8 Paul lists it with the other bodily appearances of the risen Lord.

This means that it was in the same category as the appearance of the Lord when he ate a piece of fish to demonstrate to the disciples that 'A ghost does not have flesh and bones, as you see I have' (Lk 24:39–43). It would not have helped Paul's argument for the resurrection if he had added to the appearances where the others had seen Jesus, and Thomas had even been invited to touch him, that he had had a vision! In short, he emphasizes that Jesus also appeared in bodily form to him.

He recognizes, of course, that he was in a sense different from the Twelve. Hence he uses the vivid imagery of abortion—the Greek word used in 1 Corinthians 15:8 means just that—in order to emphasize the strangeness of his appointment. However, that extraordinary appointment did not put him on a lower level or in a different category. Hence his vigorous and repeated arguments in the Corinthian letters as to the authentic nature of his apostleship: 'Am I not an apostle? Have I not seen Jesus our Lord?' (1 Cor 9:1).

His apostleship was authenticated by miraculous signs, and his special role as the apostle to the Gentiles was vindicated by the influx of Gentile believers who were the seal of his apostleship (see 1 Cor 9:2). Yet above and beyond these corroborations was the basic fact that Jesus had appeared to him.

I have often argued against Roman Catholic or Anglican views of 'bishops' as being in the so-called apostolic succession. One element in the rebuttal of their claims is the reminder that those who were eyewitnesses of the resurrection could, by definition, have no successors. They were unique to that period. I might use the same argument to my friends today who want to make Paul the prototype of a continuing apostolic office. The simple fact is that as an eyewitness of the risen Lord, he could not have a successor.

I fear that the justified reaction to the claims of some to be in the same category as Paul has obscured another question that presses in upon us if we want to be faithful to the New Testament: what do we make of the references to other apostles like Barnabas (Acts 14:4,14), James, the Lord's brother (Gal 1:19) and Andronicus and Junias (Rom 16:7)? When some of my friends react indignantly to someone's claim to be on the level of the apostle Paul I sympathize with them. I also want to guard the unique foundational position of the Twelve and Paul! However, I also want to ask who these other apostles were, and whether they have any successors. After all, the fact that there were those claiming to be apostles (Rev 2:2) but were not, indicates that there was an on-going apostolic ministry. There was also the necessity of spiritual discernment to distinguish between the genuine and the spurious. If the apostolic ministry had been confined to Paul and the Twelve, then the kind of testing implied in

Revelation 2:2 would, by definition, have been unnecessary.

If I am right that the appearance on the Damascus road was essentially an additional and unusual appearance of the risen Christ, then I need to look again at Ephesians 4. In other words, if the Twelve were appointed by the incarnate Jesus during his earthly ministry, and if the appointment of Paul really belonged to that same category in that the risen Lord appeared physically in an earthly setting, then the gift of apostles to the church in Ephesians 4 refers neither to the Twelve nor to Paul, but to those whose ministry is linked to the great gift of the ascended Lord, namely, the Holy Spirit. This would put the apostles of Ephesians 4 not only outside the unique once-for-all group, but inside the continuing ministry of the church, which embraces also prophets, evangelists and pastors/teachers.

This brings us back to the word 'apostle' itself. In the English form it could be described as a translators' 'cop-out' in that they failed to translate the Greek word *apostolos* into English, and simply dressed it up in an English form that has now become permanent. What, then, did the word mean? To answer that question is to look at the verb *apostello* from which the word *apostolos* is derived. The verb means 'to send', so that an apostle is 'a sent one'. We do have an English word that neatly fits that phrase. It comes from a Latin word, the verb *mitto*, 'to send'. The participle is *missus* ('a sent one') from which we have derived our word 'missionary'. The latter word is in fact a good translation of the word *apostolos*.

The snag is that the word missionary has itself been subject to a widening process so that it has lost something of its original thrust, when it spoke of a pioneer preacher sent to blaze a trail for the gospel. Today it is often linked with other tasks that are invaluable in the work overseas —like medical, agricultural and other auxiliary ministries

—but which are not in the strictest sense missionary tasks.

I had a most illuminating comment on this at a meeting where a doctor working in an African 'mission hospital' was speaking. He was sent out under a missionary society, and was doubtless described as a missionary. His opening words, however, struck a different note: 'I am not a missionary,' he said, 'but a doctor.'

He was making a biblical point that distinguishes the role of the deacons and deaconesses who exercise the ministry of mercy in the church and that of the preachers and teachers who are in the more directly teaching ministry. Just as the deacons' work is vitally important, so also is the 'diaconal' work overseas. It is not, however, the same ministry as that exercised by those who are called specifically to preach.

That preaching in a missionary or pioneering sense is what is implied by the word 'apostle', and is confirmed by Jesus' original call to the Twelve. Two reasons are given: 'that they might be with him and that he might send them out to preach' (Mk 3:14). The first purpose, as we have seen, was of vital importance to their unique role as foundational witnesses of the Saviour. This is one of the two qualifications mentioned in Acts 1:22. The other task is one that they shared with others like Barnabas.

It has been suggested that Barnabas was in a different category as an apostle in that he was simply a church messenger. Acts 13:1–3 should be an answer to that. The initiator of the missionary enterprise was the Holy Spirit. It is true that Saul and Barnabas were sent out by the church, but Luke recognizes the prior impulse that came from the Spirit. In that commission Paul, who already shared the special ministry of the Twelve because he was an eyewitness of the resurrection, shared also with Barnabas the missionary call to go and preach Christ where he was not already known. Hence he is Paul the apostle in the special sense of being linked with the

Twelve, and he is also in Acts 14:14 linked with Barnabas as an apostle in that he was a fellow missionary.

There is an obvious problem. In the letter to the Ephesians (2:20) Paul speaks of the church being built upon the foundation of the apostles and prophets. Does this not suggest that the apostles of the Ephesian letter are foundational? In facing that problem, my mind has gone back to Matthew 16:18 which has often been in view in my varied debates with Roman Catholics. In what sense did Jesus speak of the foundation of the church: was it Peter or Peter's testimony? The wealth of conflicting interpretations indicates how difficult the issue is, and may give us caution about being too glib in interpretating Ephesians 2:20.

I have argued (I cannot go into the argument in detail here) that it was the testimony that Peter had just given, that Jesus was the Christ, that was the foundation of the church. This would agree with Paul's insistence in 1 Corinthians 3:11 that Christ is the only foundation. So again in Ephesians, it must be the preaching of the apostles and prophets that focuses on Christ that is the basis of the church. In what sense the term 'apostles' is being used in Ephesians 2:20 is not specified. It is the preaching that is in view. To try and insist that it is the Twelve plus Paul is simply to run into further problems of understanding Revelation 21:14. One would then have to ask not only why is Paul not mentioned, but were are the prophets? I would suggest that these multiplied problems emerge from the failure to see that in Matthew 16:18, Ephesians 2:20 and Revelation 21:14 imagery is being used. The connecting theme is that of 1 Corinthians 3:11, that Jesus Christ is the one foundation. It is the preaching of the Twelve and Paul and of the other apostles and prophets, which declares that Jesus is Lord, that lies at the basis of any healthy church growth. Behind that is the witness to the earthly ministry of the Twelve recorded in the four Gospels.

A glance at Christian history will give an interesting comment on the view I have proposed that the apostles, apart from Paul and the Twelve, were essentially pioneering preachers. Christians have reacted in various centuries to outstanding missionary endeavour by using the word 'apostle' to designate the person concerned. So in the fifth century, Patrick became known as 'the apostle of Ireland', in the Reformation era, Bernard Gilpin as 'the apostle of the North' and in the nineteenth century, William Carey as the 'apostle of India'. Was this just a figurative usage of the word, or was it an instinctive recognition by Christians that such pioneers were not simply to be added to the list of great preachers or great evangelists? They were making Christ known in 'regions beyond'. They were telling out the gospel to those who had not heard.

There is one further unresolved problem as far as I am concerned in my attempts to understand the New Testament in this matter. It is the ministry of James, the Lord's brother. He was certainly not one of the Twelve, for, after all, during the Lord's ministry his brothers did not accept him. Yet Paul in Galatians 1:19 clearly refers to him as an apostle. The problem is that in the references to him in the New Testament he appears more in the role of presiding leader of the church in Jerusalem.

This occurs in Paul's reference in Galatians 1. It is even more apparent in the account given in Acts 15 of the gathering in Jerusalem. The vexed issue of whether or not Gentile believers were to be circumcised was being debated. While both Paul and Peter were present, it was James who presided, and when the decree was issued it was in his name that it went.

Clearly James was in a very eminent position. He had been one of the witnesses of the resurrection (1 Cor 15:7) and in the reference to him in Galatians 2:9 he appears first in the list of three who welcomed Paul to Jerusalem. Yet all the references speak of him as located in Jerusalem. The early church historian Eusebius quotes from the Memoir of Hegesippus, who lived in the second century. Here we read that James held the government of the church along with the apostles. At the end of the first century Josephus, the Jewish historian, recalled the killing of James, which took place after the death of Festus before whom Paul had appeared. His martyrdom happened in the late sixties A.D. and Josephus reckoned its cruel injustice as being one of the causes of the seige of Jerusalem, which fell in 70 A.D.

A tentative answer may be offered to the question as to the nature of James' apostolic ministry, in that he seems to have been localized at Jerusalem. There is the fact that Hegesippus links his martyrdom with his fearless testimony to Jesus as the Son of God. It is a reminder that Jerusalem was itself a hostile mission field, and while the others might range widely in their apostolic preaching, James was challenging the very citadel of Judaism and paying for it with his life.

It may also be that James is a reminder that the missionary preachers blazing a trail for the gospel were not concerned simply with seeing converts emerge. They had a further task, namely, the establishing of each new church on biblical lines. So Paul and Barnabas go out on their apostolic journeys to preach. Then they return to appoint elders and to see how the churches are progressing. Similarly, Paul aims to visit Rome, where there was already a fellowship of believers, in order to contribute to them and then to press on with his pioneering to fields beyond.

The various ministries in the New Testament are not defined in such clear-cut terms that there was no overlap. There is no hint of a demarcation procedure as in some industrial situations today! So Peter can refer to himself as 'a fellow elder' (1 Pet 5:1) and Paul can urge Timothy to do the work of an evangelist (2 Tim 4:5). The ministry of Titus is not designated by a title, yet he appears to be acting with the same kind of authority as Barnabas and Paul when going authoritatively to churches in every town to ordain elders. There was, however, in every ministry a twofold aim—to declare the lordship of Jesus Christ and to establish churches that were true to the word and submissive to the Holy Spirit.

12

Prophets and Prophecy

To suggest even the possibility that prophecy is a continuing gift within the church is to invite a strong reaction. Surely, the objector will urge, the canon of Scripture is closed. The completion of the New Testament gave the final revelation of which Hebrews 1:1 spoke so clearly. Since God has spoken decisively and finally in the apostolic testimony to Christ, it is not only foolish to expect further revelations, but more seriously it is a rejection of the basic Christian assertion of the sufficiency of Holy Scripture. To have an open-ended revelation is to throw the door wide for all the aberrations of Christian history from the vision of Bernadette Soubirois at Lourdes to the claims to new revelations by Joseph Smith and the Mormons.

At the other extreme there is a different kind of reaction. It is to welcome the possibility with delight, and even with excitement. Any claim to speak directly from the Lord is willingly accepted. Any prediction spoken with an air of authority must, it is assumed, be authentic, and therefore demands assent and submission. The fact that some of these predictions are subsequently proved false is forgotten in the general fever of enthusiasm. The further fact that others are little more than generalized observation or devotional comment is also ignored. Those who are on an emotional high neither wait for the sobering reality of experience nor the critical assessment by Scripture. Yet it is precisely these that are urgently needed.

Both reactions need to be brought under the scrutiny of Scripture. Since the basic conviction of this present book is that the Spirit of truth is the giver of every spiritual gift, then his own clear testimony in Scripture must be our criterion for testing every claim to authority, and every particular utterance that purports to be authentic.

Let me, then, reiterate at the outset of this discussion of prophecy my own basic conviction that Scripture is God's final and sufficient revelation. I do not believe in an open-ended Bible. I accept the historic contention that the canon is closed. The sufficiency of Scripture is my basic starting point. This, however, does not mean that the understanding of Scripture is final at any given point in the individual's life, nor indeed at any point of Christian history. Scripture is complete but our appreciation and grasp of it are always, or should always be, growing.

It may also be appropriate to point out that some who display a great concern when prophecy is mentioned react in a different way when preaching is under discussion. If the sufficiency of Scripture was to be interpreted in the rigid way that their reaction to the mention of prophecy suggests, they should not do anything in the pulpit but read the Scriptures. Certainly they should not claim to have in the pulpit a preacher of the word of God. A rigid interpretation of sufficiency would preclude such preaching since it would be additional to the actual words of Scripture.

Furthermore, in the area of counselling their view of sufficiency will lead to strange results if rigorously applied. Thus a preacher tells his congregation that he is persuaded that God is calling him to Africa, and so he will be leaving for missionary service. But where did he find Zaïre or Angola mentioned by name in the Bible? He claims that he has been given an overwhelmingly direct mandate from the Holy Spirit, yet in this he is gloriously inconsistent.

In fact, he will probably respond by pointing to the Scriptures themselves where preaching is clearly declared as being central to the life of the church, and where personal guidance by direct constraint of the Spirit is also revealed. I would wholeheartedly agree, but would point out that in his admissions about preaching and guidance, which I willingly share, he is indicating a view of the sufficiency of Scripture that leaves the issue of prophecy an open one. In short, we can discuss the subject without being accused of incipient liberalism or some subtle attempt to undermine the canon of Scripture.

In an earlier chapter, I argued from the prophecy of Joel, recalled in Acts 2, for the continuance of prophecy in the church. It is important, however, to qualify this in view of the other over-reaction, which has caused concern to those contending for the sufficiency of Scripture, namely, the credulity that accepts every claim uncritically and rather feverishly anticipates more exciting revelations to come. To guard against both, I return again to Paul's double warning in 1 Thessalonians 5:19–21: 'Do not put out the Spirit's fire; do not treat prophecies with contempt. Test everything.' We must be prepared to listen when the Spirit speaks. At the same time we must be ready to test whether the utterance is truly from the Spirit and not just from the lips of the person who speaks, or indeed from some demonic agency using human lips.

Paul makes the same point in different ways in 1 Corinthians 12:3 and in 14:37–38. In the first of these references Paul rejects the utterance 'Jesus be cursed.' This may have come from some unbalanced zealot who was misapplying the truth that at Calvary Jesus became a curse for us (Gal 3:13) or it may have been due to a demonic manipulation of the speaker. Whatever the explanation, such an utterance cannot be from the Spirit since his ministry is to glorify Jesus as Christ the Lord. Tested by the truth of Scripture, such a word must be rejected.

This has a much wider application than the specific example quoted here. Claims have been made in Roman Catholic circles that they have been prompted by the Holy Spirit in extolling Mary. To say this is to run completely counter to the Spirit's testimony in the Bible. Jesus alone is to be glorified. He alone is mediator. He alone is the one through whom we come to the Father, and he has sufficient sympathy to enter into our petitions. The 'hail Marys' of the rosary, the false notion of Mary as the mother of the church as taught by the Second Vatican Council, together with all the other false ideas about Mary, founder on the rock of Scripture. To claim the Spirit's prompting or to assert prophetic authority is to be rejected out of hand by the Spirit of truth.

In the second quotation (1 Cor 14:37–38) Paul is making the same basic point. He has been urging the church in Corinth to listen to the prophets, and so to be ready to obey them. Yet this listening is not to be uncritical. They are to be tested, as Paul himself had once been tested in Berea by the Old Testament Scriptures (Acts 17:11). Now Paul himself is writing Scripture just as the Old Testamant authors wrote. In both cases the end product is the command of the Lord. Let the prophets in Corinth—and every other prophet of every other generation—recognize that the divinely-given apostolic testimony is the touchstone of truth. By that testimony their prophetic words are to be tested and either endorsed or repudiated.

There are further tests to be employed, both of these

being derived from the basic criterion of Scripture. There is the objective assessment of any utterance that has a predictive element. Deuteronomy 18:20–22 gave that and also the sentence to be imposed. If the prediction did not come to pass then the alleged prophecy was presumptuous. God did not command it. The man who had thus deceived his hearers was to be stoned—it was the outward sign of complete rejection. The New Testament equivalent of this would seem to be total exclusion from the Christian fellowship. In a day when predictive utterances have been all too lightly given, this is a very sobering reminder that the subsequent proof that they are unfounded brings great spiritual peril.

The further test emerges in the list of gifts given in 1 Corinthians 12. Alongside the gift of prophecy is the complementary gift of the ability to distinguish between spirits (verse 10). Spiritual discernment is not simply the outcome of study or of experience, though both of these are valuable contributory factors. It is ultimately a gift from the Holy Spirit. The very fact that such a gift is necessary indicates that the claim to prophetic utterance does not automatically guarantee that that claim is valid. On the other hand, if there is no such gift as prophecy today, such a discerning gift would not be needed.

Turning, then, more directly to the nature of prophecy and the role of the prophet, it is important to notice the difference between someone to whom God gives a gift of prophecy, and one who is regularly used by God in a prophetic ministry. Indeed, the office of the prophet in the church is described in Ephesians 4 as being itself a gift from the ascended Lord who has, in the giving of the Spirit to the church, given various preaching and teaching gifts for the building up of his people.

A gift of prophecy may only be given in an occasional way. In the case of King Saul it seems to have been a once-only bestowal. The question that was asked by the astonished onlookers indicates the distinction between such a special donation by God and the regular pattern of prophetic ministry: 'Is Saul also among the prophets?' (1 Sam 19:24). The words he spoke were clearly from the Lord. Yet this did not make him a prophet. In the same way, Paul urges the Corinthians to seek the gift of prophecy. Yet this did not mean that the whole of the church was to be comprised of prophets. This is confirmed by the fact that in the church in Antioch (Acts 13:1–3) there was within the fellowship a clearly defined body of prophets.

Within Scripture, both in the Old and the New Testaments, there are different levels of prophecy. There were those in the Old Testament whose prophecies were for the people of God in every subsequent generation. Such were therefore, by the Spirit's impulse (2 Pet 1:19–21), recorded in written form as authoritative Scripture, on a level with the law of Moses. There were also many prophets like the one hundred whom Obadiah hid in the cave (1 Kings 18:13). Their message was clearly from God, or they would not have been given the title, yet their words were not recorded. Their utterances must have had an immediate reference for those to whom they spoke. Yet their words did not have the abiding significance of those that came through the canonical prophets like Isaiah, Hosea and the others.

It must be recalled that there is a substantial period of time—something like three centuries—between the last prophet of the Old Testament and when John the Baptist began to preach and so fulfil the prophecy of Malachi. During that period, the Jewish rabbis reflected on the Old Testament, and wrote much in order to expound the sacred Scriptures. It was also the period of apocalyptic writing, the roots of which were in the Old Testament, but whose speculations about the future were tinged by the turbulent days through which many of the writers passed.

While we do not attribute to such writings of the inter-testamental period the authority that belongs to Scripture, they are none the less valuable. On the one hand, they show how Jewish thinking was being influenced. They also illustrate how particular words were being employed. When we reflect further on the fact that the writers of the New Testament books were the final generation of that inter-testamental period, and Paul himself was schooled in rabbinic writings, we will notice the way in which a word such as 'prophecy' is used. That does not mean that the New Testament writers used this term or any other in an identical way. It does, however, give us valuable clues as to the background meaning of words that were already current coin in religious writing.

Wayne Grudem in his very valuable work on prophecy in 1 Corinthians has some useful comments on this matter of contemporary usage.[12] He points out that while, on the one side there is an acknowledgement that prophecy in its canonical sense as the authoritative word of God had ceased, yet Jewish writers of this period believed that God continued to speak to men. They had a very high view of Old Testament prophecy as being the very words of God given through the lips of inspired men who could claim 'Thus saith the Lord'. Their message, therefore, and their precise words demanded submission. At the same time there was a recognition that men still spoke from God. Yet their words did not have the absolute authority of the Old Testament prophets. They were to be listened to and obeyed but only in so far as they conformed to the truths declared in the Old Testament writings. Just as we may hear the word of the Lord through a preacher anointed by the Spirit, or through a piece of Christian literature, so they would have claimed to have heard God's word. Yet in the testing of preaching and literature today, and in their assessment of rabbinic writing, the final court of appeal is now and was then, the supreme authority of the Bible.

There was thus a distinction that Grudem notices between the word that was authoritative both in its message and in all its constituent words—to such prophecy there must be unqualified submission—and the message that is authoritative in its general content, but the specific arguments or actual words of which must be scrutinized in the light of Scripture, and as a result may be modified.

The term 'prophecy' was thus used in different senses. It could refer to the infallible oracles of the Old Testament. It could also refer to the utterances and writings of godly men whose words had to be tested. It is the difference between Prophecy with a capital 'P' and prophecy with a lower case 'p'. The question, however, then arises: do the New Testament writers themselves draw this distinction between two levels of prophecy? It is one thing to acknowledge that they were the heirs of their own religious, cultural and linguistic traditions. It is quite another thing to assert that in their own writings they use an inherited terminology in the same sense. To prove that in the case of prophecy they did so, we must examine the actual teaching of the New Testament authors themselves.

It is certainly very clear that the New Testament writers recognize the unique authority of the prophets of the Old Testament. They echo the attitude of Jesus who not only quoted frequently from the Old Testament but insisted in the most unequivocal statement he made on the subject that 'the Scripture cannot be broken' (Jn 10:35). What is required, therefore, in the face of Scripture is unqualified obedience.

The New Testament writers go further and both implicitly and explicity put their own writings on the same level as Old Testament Scripture. We have noticed already how Paul states in 1 Corinthians 14:37 that his words are the final court of appeal. Similarly, when Peter refers to Paul's letters he puts them in the same bracket as 'the other Scriptures' (2 Pet 3:16). When Luke introduces his Gospel, his declared aim is to give 'certainty'—the Latin version significantly translated the Greek term by *infallibilitas*.

One can only conclude that the foundational apostles of the New Testament were the true fulfilment of the Old Testament prophets. Paul, for example, insists that his authority is neither conferred by men nor derived from them but comes directly from God (Gal 1:1; see also Rom 1:1; 2 Cor 1:1). He and his fellows are the ministers of the new covenant standing on a level with Moses, the minister of the old covenant, which they now declare to be fulfilled in Christ (2 Cor 3:6–18).

One can, therefore, appreciate the contrast in the attitude that is to be adopted to the continuing prophets in the church. In the extended treatment of the matter in 1 Corinthians 14, the basic theme is that their words are to be tested. It is not the prophets themselves who are to be tested. They are already accepted as prophets by the church in Corinth. They are not, therefore, like visiting prophets whose credentials have to be assessed as John asserts (1 Jn 4:1,3; 2 Jn 10). It is thus their teaching that is to be weighed up; in 1 Corinthians 14:29 the Greek verb used suggests a careful evaluation by a discerning people.

The prophecy in the New Testament could also have a personal and local application. Thus Paul recalls the prophecy that was given when Timothy was ordained to the ministry of the word. Clearly it had an authority for Timothy as being a word from the Lord. There is, however, no indication of its content. It did not have a general application. The fact that it was given was significant, but the content was personal and local. It did not apply to a wider audience, witness the silence of the Spirit-led author of 2 Timothy. Hence, one can understand how a word delivered today in a local church may have a message for that church, but is not of general application. Once again one is seeing the fact of two levels of prophecy —the infallible biblical oracle and the occasional personal or local message. The former is to be received both 'in word and words', the latter 'in word only', to use Grudem's useful distinction.

This may be an appropriate point to comment on the custom in some circles for a purported prophecy to be introduced by the phrase 'Thus saith the Lord' and to be continued in the first person singular, e.g. 'I say to you . . . I tell you,' etc. This I believe to be not only misleading but also spiritually harmful. It obscures the fundamental distinction between infallible Scripture and a contemporary word that must be tested by Scripture. To use the introduction 'Thus saith the Lord' is to identify the utterance with that of the Old Testament prophets who used precisely that introduction. To speak in the first person singular is to claim implicitly, as the prophets of Scripture certainly did, that the words being given are in fact the words of the Lord himself. This surely means that the contemporary prophecy is claiming to be infallible and supremely authoritative. Indeed it makes the whole process of testing such utterance, as laid down in 1 Corinthians 14, completely irrelevant. If, in fact, the Corinthian prophets were to be tested by Scripture, then it is grievous presumption for anyone today to present themselves as being on a level with Scripture and thus above being tested or challenged. The harm such presumption does is compounded by the fact that, not surprisingly, it leads some who correctly recognize how wrong it is, to react to the opposite extreme, dismissing all who teach the continuance of prophecy in the church as if they belonged in the same category.

To return to the main theme a further issue must be raised, namely, the predictive element of prophecy. To suggest that some prophecies may have no predictive element in them is to face the charge of denial of the supernatural in Scripture. In reply one must point to the declared purposes of the kind of prophecy under discussion in 1 Corinthians 14. In verse 3 Paul states the aims. They have nothing to do with foretelling the future. They are given, rather, with a view to 'strengthening, encouragement and comfort.' John Calvin's comment is worth recording at this point. In his commentary on 1 Corinthians he refers to this phrase and adds:

> I am certain in my own mind that he means by prophets, not those endowed with a gift of foretelling, but those who were blessed with the unique gift of dealing with Scripture not only by interpreting it, but also by the wisdom they showed in making it meet the need of the hour.

Such a view of the prophet puts him firmly in the ranks of the proclaimers. This would accord with Ephesians 4 in which the prophet is distinct from the teacher, though, as in other offices in the New Testament, there is no rigid demarcation of the differences between the different roles. Peter, for example, though one of the twelve apostles, also designates himself as an elder (1 Pet 5:1). While a man's primary office might be clear, this did not preclude him from sharing in some other ministries. Thus, a man may be primarily a preacher and yet may be a fellow elder with others who, together with him, exercise pastoral oversight of the congregation.

In reformed circles where there has been a high view of the ministerial office, there has also been an insistence on the plurality of elders within a local church. Appeal has been made to 1 Timothy 5:17 to draw a distinction between teaching and ruling elders. This does not seem to me to be a valid distinction since a basic qualification for every elder is being 'able to teach' (1 Tim 3:2). In any case, the reference in 1 Timothy 5:17 is to those elders whose work is a full-time commitment, which thus requires financial support from the congregation. Yet an elder might not have a preaching gift and might none the less have such an aptitude for teaching that he is set apart from his ordinary work to engage in a teaching and pastoral ministry within the fellowship.

If Calvin is correct in seeing in 1 Corinthians 14:3 a preacher, and if this also is the essential character of the prophet or proclaimer of Ephesians 4, then we have in the latter chapter not a list of offices with one office retained (the pastor/teacher), one possibly retained (the evangelist) and two perhaps or perhaps not! Rather, we have the continuing pattern for the regular life of the church. There are the missionary pioneers, the preachers, the preachers with a special evangelistic gift, and the pastors/teachers.

Preaching, after all, is not simply the eloquent presentation of a well-prepared statement of some area of Christian truth. Paul spoke with a demonstration of the Spirit's power (1 Cor 2:4). Reference is often made to a preacher having 'an anointing'. Sometimes the recognition of such divine unction is applied to the preaching itself. A preacher himself knows when he is simply presenting a well-prepared, logically-reasoned and aptly-illustrated sermon, and when he is enjoying the liberty of the Spirit. There is a deep sense in which he is only truly preaching when there is that anointing of the Spirit.

Other descriptions of the preacher point to a similar conclusion. He is the herald (Greek *kerux*). The oriental monarch of the first century announced his arrival in a town or village by the trumpet blast of his herald. So also the King of kings awakens sinners and summons saints to worship and service by the Spirit's trumpeter, the anointed proclaimer of the word.

There is an interesting comment on all this in one of the earliest pieces of Christian literature after the period of the New Testament. The *Didache*[13] (the Greek word means 'teaching') dates from around the year 100 A.D. so it represents the pattern of life familiar to many whose lives overlapped the lifetime of at least one of the Twelve, the apostle John, if not some of the others. While clearly it does not have the authority of Scripture, it is particularly significant in showing how the first generation after the apostles applied Scripture to church life.

There are vigorous reminders of the importance of testing the claims of itinerant prophets: 'Not every one that speaketh in the spirit is a prophet, but if he have the manners of the Lord' (11:8). There is a wary attitude to those who seem less concerned with their message than with their monetary reward: 'if he asks money he is a false prophet ... And no prophet that orders a table in the spirit shall eat of it, else he is a false prophet. And every prophet that teacheth the truth if he doest not what he teacheth is a false prophet' (11:6, 9,10).

Of particular interest, in view of the suggestion in this chapter that the prophet and the pastor/teacher continue today, is the reference to this very pattern within a few years of the death of the last of the Twelve. Thus there is reference not only to the itinerant prophets who pay a brief visit to a congregation, but also to a prophet who settles down and is maintained by the gifts of the congregation. His ministry does not preclude or override the other regular ministries. So the *Didache* lays down the following directions: 'But every true prophet who is minded to settle among you is worthy of his maintenance. In like manner a true teacher also is worthy, like every workman, of his maintenance ... Elect therefore for yourselves bishops and deacons worthy of the Lord, men meek and not covetous, and true and approved, for they also minister unto you the ministry of the prophets and teachers' (13:1; 15:1).

Returning to Paul's treatment of prophecy and

prophets in 1 Corinthians 14, it is set in the context of his teaching on 'speaking in a tongue'. I will deal with this gift later, but since it is impossible to deal with prophecy in 1 Corinthians 14 without reference to 'tongues', there will inevitably be some anticipation at this point. A basic consideration that colours much of the discussion of both of these gifts is the distinction that Paul emphasizes in 14:2–3. The utterance in a 'tongue' is directed towards God and is emphatically 'not to men'. Prophecy, by contrast, is directed towards men. That is why the person who speaks in a tongue only edifies himself whereas the one who prophesies edifies the church.

This is also the reason why Paul sets prophecy on a much higher level than speaking in a tongue. It is not that he denigrates the latter. Indeed, he not only rejoices in his claim 'I speak in tongues more than all of you' (1 Cor 14:18), but he also expresses a keen desire: 'I would like every one of you to speak in tongues' (1 Cor 14:5). He also warns against any rejection of this gift: 'Do not forbid speaking in tongues' (1 Cor 14:39). His reason, therefore, for extolling prophecy as superior is in no way because of any undervaluing of the gift of tongues. It is simply that prophecy, being an intelligible word, builds up the church. It is only when an utterance in a tongue is accompanied by an interpretation that it also is accepted and indeed valued in the public use since it now also edifies others.

The gift of prophecy is thus the imparting of the ability to receive a message from the Lord and so to declare it to men and women that it will bring to them the realization that God has spoken. This means that three elements will be present. It will accord with Scripture, to which every prophetic utterance is subject and by which it must be judged. Secondly, it will honour the Lord Jesus Christ who, as the ascended Lord, has given his Spirit to his people. The Spirit thus imparts the gift of prophecy that the glory of Christ may be manifest within the church. Thirdly, it will come with such authority to those who hear that it will elicit a response of repentance and faith, and so will lead to worship. Thus, even the outsider who comes under the power of a prophetic word will, in Paul's words, 'be convinced by all [that is, all who are prophesying] that he is a sinner and will be judged by all, and the secrets of his heart will be laid bare. So he will fall down and worship God, exclaiming, "God is really among you!"' (1 Cor 14:24–25).

Every prophecy is to be tested. Even in the case of the occasional utterance, there is still need for spiritual evaluation. As we saw earlier, Paul lays down as a qualification of the acceptance of prophecy the necessity to prove all things (1 Thess 5:21). We also noted that the gift of prophecy has alongside it the gift of discernment, which enables those so gifted to assess whether a prophetic word is truly from the Lord (1 Cor 12:10). This constant assessment is all the more needed when it is not the occasional utterance of a member of the congregation that is in view, but the regular ministry of one who is recognized as a prophet. In view of his authoritative ministry in the church, bestowed as it has been by the Holy Spirit, there is always the danger of people almost automatically assuming that the prophet must be accepted and every utterance obeyed. Hence, Paul lays down very firmly the principles that should govern the assessment of his ministry.

There should be personal discipline and self-control on the part of the prophet. He is not in some kind of emotional state so that he cannot but utter what is in his mind. 'The spirits of prophets are subject to the control of prophets' (1 Cor 14:32). To have a total lack of restraint would be a prescription for chaos. God, however, as Paul clearly points out, 'is not a God of disorder but of peace' (verse 33). This means that in a shared ministry situation such as Paul envisaged at Corinth, one prophet must be prepared to give way to another one when there is the witness of the Spirit that the latter has a fresh word from the Lord.

When a message was given, it was to be weighed up carefully (1 Cor 14:29). It is not totally clear who it is that is to do the weighing. Is it the other prophets or the whole congregation? The former would seem more likely for two reasons. The congregation as a whole would embrace both mature Christians and very recent converts who would not be in a position to evaluate how biblical a message was. Then again, the very definiteness of the phrase 'the others' suggests strongly that it is the other prophets.

This interpretation of the phrase 'the others' as a reference to the other prophets is reinforced by the insistence in verses 34–35 that the women should keep silent. This cannot mean a total ban or it would preclude their joining in praise! Furthermore the reference in 1 Corinthians 11:5 speaks of women 'prophesying' and the context of that passage semes clearly to be a full service of worship with men and women present. The silence here in 14:35 is in the context of judging the utterances of the prophets. Such would involve exercising authority over men and this would violate the principle laid down in 1 Timothy 2:11–14. The prohibition of questions in this context is also understandable—any who have listened to a parliamentary question time will know that a question may not really be a request for information but an indirect way of making a point!

The word translated 'weigh' is the verbal form of the same word that appears as a noun in 1 Corinthians 12:10, where it is translated in the Revised Version as 'discernings'. In the latter case, the plural form suggests a wider ability in the area of discernment. It would appear to be descriptive of the ability to discern whether the one who speaks is doing so under the direction of the Holy Spirit or through the agency of an evil spirit. It is used in this wider sense in a variety of ways in the New Testament. Thus, Paul discerned in the case of Elymas in Cyprus (Acts 13:8–11) and the girl in Philippi (Acts 16:16–18) that the origin of their utterances was satanic. It is in this sense that Jesus himself discerned the source of some incidents of sickness (Lk 13:16). Similarly, in 1 John 4:1 it is the claims to being prophets that are to be tested.

Here in 1 Corinthians 14:29 it is the message itself that is to be assessed. The word implies an evaluation and a judgement as to whether a statement is to be accepted or not, or whether it is to be accepted in general terms while receiving either slight or marked qualification as far as detail is concerned. Thus, in the evaluation of the statement 'Jesus be cursed' (1 Cor 12:3) total rejection is the result. Where however, as in 1 Corinthians 14:29, there is an implied general acceptance, there is also quite definitely an assessment and a judgement that might, therefore, mean a modified acceptance.

We are familiar enough with that kind of assessment in relation to preaching. The hearer may come into a service of worship with a whole-hearted concern to listen to the preaching, with an honest and submissive desire to hear the word of the Lord. He may, indeed, be greatly blessed whether by rebuke, encouragement or challenge. He may be profoundly grateful that he is under the authority of a preacher sent from God. Yet he does not become a mere 'yes man'. He does not confer infallibility on the preacher's utterance. He recognizes that a man may truly be anointed by the Spirit and will yet still be a finite creature with evidence not only of limitations but also of indwelling sinfulness. Yet he rejoices that, in spite of human frailty, the preacher brings such a message that he can respond with the testimony, 'God spoke to me today!'

Now the fact that the prophetic utterances in Corinth

were thus to be assessed and judged indicates that they were viewed as not being on the same level as Scripture. In the latter case, as we have already seen, the attitude is not one of discerning and judging, but that of acceptance and submission. Indeed, in this very chapter the apostolic testimony of the author of this area of Scripture is on a different level. Paul does not call them to weigh or judge his word from the Lord. Rather, in verse 37 it is this word that is to be used in judging the prophets of Corinth.

While the general pattern of 1 Corinthians 14 presents prophecy primarily as proclamation, it would be thoroughly unbiblical to ignore the predictive element in prophecy. There are clear illustrations of this in the book of Acts, with Agabus as a notable example. He foretold the severe famine that subsequently took place during the reign of Claudius (Acts 11:28). He also predicted Paul's imprisonment in Judea, which duly happened (Acts 21:10–11). Paul himself predicted the survival of the entire ship's company in the shipwreck off Malta (Acts 27:34).

Similar predictions can be quoted from Christian history. In the famous account of the Covenanters, *The Scots Worthies*, among various pieces of evidence of supernatural happening there are the extraordinary predictions of Alexander Peden. One who in many ways stood in the same tradition as the Covenanters, C. H. Spurgeon, recalls something similar in his autobiography. It happened when he was a very small boy. The prediction was specific: 'This boy will one day preach in Rowland Hill's chapel.' No one could have known by human intuition that the little boy would become the great preacher. But God knew it and revealed it.

In this area of prediction we find further support for the main thesis of this chapter, namely, that there are two levels of prophecy and of prophets. There is the infallible and universally binding prophecy of Scripture and there is the prophecy that truly reveals something from the Lord but does not have the infallibility of Scripture. To employ Grudem's useful distinction again, there is Prophecy that is authoritative in word and in words, and prophecy that is authoritative in word, that is, in general content but which must be weighed as to its detailed words.

It is appropriate here to examine the prophecy of Agabus concerning Paul's imprisonment. Certainly it was true in its essential message that Paul would be rejected by the Jews and imprisoned by the Romans. However, a close examination of the details of Agabus' words recorded under divine inspiration by Luke do not match Luke's detailed account of what actually happened. Thus Agabus foretold that the Jews would bind the hands of the apostle and hand him over to the Romans. In Acts 21:30 the Jewish mob seized Paul and tried to kill him. Far from handing him over to the Romans they demonstrated lynch law in action. Indeed, the Romans actually rescued Paul from the Jews. Further, although Paul was bound by the Romans with two chains, Luke notes that his hands were free so that he could use them in his characteristic manner when addressing a public meeting—he 'motioned to the crowd' (Acts 21:40).

What I am doing here is precisely what Paul urged should be done in Corinth. I am using the infallible Scripture penned by Luke, the author of Acts, to assess the detail of the prophetic word delivered by Agabus. In like manner, the prophets of Corinth were to be heeded as God's messengers, but the details of their messages were subject to the higher authority of the apostolic testimony.

13

Tongues

Paul's concern was not with theoretical discussion of interesting doctrinal issues but with the life of the church. His concern for his converts was that they should be gathered into local churches. There they would grow spiritually, and in fellowship and shared worship they would glorify their Lord. From that living base they would reach out to others who were without God and without hope because they were without Christ. That is still the pattern for today.

His great treatment of the 'gift of tongues' is thus set in the context of his concern to regulate the worship of the church in Corinth. Among the other sorry evidence of doctrinal and moral failure in Corinth, the disfigurement of worship was all too obvious. There was exhibitionism, a feverish appetite for excitement and, above all, a self-centred forgetfulness that the worship in a local church is not designed for individualistic self-satisfaction, or personal display. Rather, it is to be a shared experience of mutual delight in the grace of God, and mutual concern for the spiritual welfare of the whole fellowship.

Paul, however, does not react with either an excessively negative or a legalistic approach. There is no prescription here for a liturgical strait-jacket. The answer to licence is not a detailed list of precise rules, but a pattern of ordered liberty. Thus, he avoids both an authoritarian control of worship by the leadership and a free-for-all that leads to chaos. His basic principle is that 'Everything should be done in a fitting and orderly way' (1 Cor 14:40) but letting the liberty of the Spirit be realized within that framework. It is in the context of disciplined freedom that he considers the matter of 'speaking in a tongue'.

The first step in examining the teaching is to ask two questions that are closely related: In what sense is the word 'tongue' used and are the tongues whose use is described in Acts 2 the same as those described in 1 Corinthians 14? Clearly, in both situations people were uttering sounds that in no way corresponded with their own native language or dialect, yet at the same time those sounds were meaningful to at least some of those who heard them. Were they, then, words in a language foreign to the speaker yet intelligible to the hearer, either because of a supernatural intervention in the process of hearing, or in an equally miraculous bestowal of the ability of someone to translate? In short, the two basic questions lead to a variety of subsidiary questions. Let's begin with the basic ones!

The word 'tongue' is normally used in two senses. It refers to the physical organ in the mouth that is our instrument for producing intelligible speech. It is also used in a derived sense for the resulting language that is produced. So we speak of the wagging tongue of the gossip, or the glib tongue of the clever salesman. We also refer to someone after years abroad finding great relief in returning home to speak in his own native tongue. Similarly, someone whose work necessitates the constant use of a second language refers to his own mother tongue. So 'tongue', where it is not specifically referring to the physical organ, indicates a spoken language.

While we use the word normally to refer to a spoken language, it is clear that the physical tongue that is normally used to produce intelligible speech may also be used to produce gibberish. Someone who is suffering from brain damage, from over-emotional excitement, from hysteria or from drunkenness may pour out a flood of what is really a verbal jumble. So also in the exercise of occult power, someone may utter what is unintelligible. We must, therefore, ask whether the utterances described in Acts 2 and 1 Corinthians 14 were this kind of ecstatic speech that could not really be designated as a language.

It is important to digress at this point and emphasize what has already been underlined at an earlier stage of this book. We are discussing at the moment the 'tongues' of the New Testament. Too often the whole issue is side-tracked by a premature reference to contemporary claims, and to assertions by professional linguists that they have not found in the tape recordings that they have examined any recognizable language structure. To whatever conclusion we may come on current claims or rebuttals, our starting point must be the New Testament evidence.

One general observation must be made on the phenomena in Acts 2 and 1 Corinthians 14, leaving aside for the moment the question whether or not they are the same: it is that sense cannot be elicited from nonsense. Gibberish such as may pour from the lips of a brain-damaged or a hysterical person remains a jumble of sounds. They are without sense or meaning. If, however, the end result is an intelligible utterance to at least some hearers—as it was on the day of Pentecost and at Corinth —then if the original sounds were not a language, the translated utterance can have no relationship to what was uttered in the first place. Yet in Corinth at least Paul is using the word 'translate' or 'interpret' to describe the transition from the unknown to the known. Such a reference to translating is valid when, for example, a Chinese or a Swahili utterance is presented intelligibly to an English speaker who knows neither of these tongues. It began as 'sense', although unknown in the foreign tongue. It reappears as 'sense' in the known language of the hearer. If, however, it started its career as gibberish, that is, as nonsense, it could not by any means or assistance make the leap to sense or intelligibility.

Yet there is more specific evidence that the tongue in both passages is a language. In Acts 2 it seems abundantly clear that they were actual languages that were being spoken. Thus in verses 6 and 8 the hearers referred to the words they heard as being spoken in the various dialects, and in verse 11 they equate these with 'our own tongues'. So 'tongue' is clearly used interchangeably for 'dialect' or 'vernacular'. It is obviously a spoken language.

In verse 4, Luke uses the same word to describe their utterance when speaking in tongues as he uses in verse 14 in reference to Peter's preaching. In the latter case Peter is using Greek, the customary language around the Mediterranean. The utterance thus quite obviously refers to a language being spoken. Surely, then, in verse 4 it was also a language that was being articulated, although in this case it was a foreign tongue as far as the speaker was concerned.

While the tongues were understandable to those who spoke the particular languages being used, this was far from obvious to all. Luke records the contemptuous dismissal of the whole affair by those who reckoned that the speakers had had much too much to drink. To them it sounded like the incoherent rubbish that a hopelessly drunk man may pour out. On the other hand, to the ears of those for whom the utterance was their own mother tongue it was not rambling nonsense, but a clear burst of praise describing the wonderful works of God.

There were others who were more discerning, yet they

were still perplexed. The Greek word that Luke uses here suggests a state of utter amazement. They were overwhelmed with amazement. These men to whom they were listening were Galileans. They would have the pronounced accent of northerners. It was like someone from Surrey listening to a Liverpudlian. The sophisticated audience recognized that the Galilean provincials were not widely-travelled men. They were in no position to acquire the varied dialects spoken in different parts of Asia Minor and the Mediterranean lands. Yet here was the incredible fact that, without either tuition or previous practice, they were praising God in languages not their own. It is no wonder that they were ready to listen to Peter's explanation as he reverted to everyday Greek.

There has, however, been a totally different interpretation of the passage which maintains that the miracle was not in the area of speech but of hearing. This is no recent theory for its roots go back to the early centuries of the Christian church, at least as far back as the time of Gregory Nazianzus in the fourth century. Those who adopt this interpretation contend that it was in the minds of the hearers that the Holy Spirit worked the miracle. So, in fact, it is argued, the disciples were still speaking with their strong Galilean accents, but the crowd heard them in their own various dialects.

This certainly would be a convenient way of avoiding questions about the nature of the tongues. It would also cut any link between the events on the day of Pentecost and the phenomena of Corinth, since in the latter case the tongues were certainly located not in the hearing of the worshippers but in the voice of the speakers, witness the obvious ability to use them in private when no one else would be listening. However, I believe the theory is completely untenable for various reasons.

In the first place there is Luke's explicit statement that they 'Began to speak in other tongues as the Spirit enabled them' (Acts 2:4). Furthermore, the initial speaking preceded the hearing and, indeed, there was an interval between the first outburst of speech and the subsequent arrival of the excited crowd. The disciples were indoors when the Spirit was poured out and the gift of tongues bestowed (verse 2). They must then have moved into the open or into the temple courts. A crowd soon gathered, perplexed by the extraordinary reports that were speedily being relayed around the city. There was thus a time gap, short though it may have been, before the outsiders gathered to listen to the bursts of praise. These had already been poured out in the house where the audience was not multi-racial nor multi-lingual, but essentially provincial and Galilean, and above all actually participating: 'All of them were filled with the Holy Spirit and began to speak in other tongues as the Spirit enabled them' (verse 4). So, prior to the arrival of hearers, the tongues were being used, and at that stage there were no spectators to hear them, only active speakers to utter them!

An attempt to bolster the theory is to employ as a counter-argument the fact that some of the crowd did not hear languages but only the incoherent jumble of what they claimed was drunken gibberish. That, however, is a weak objection. Those who accused the disciples of being drunk were clearly hostile critics. But hostility can seriously impair a person's judgement. Take the case of Paul's appearance before Festus. To read Paul's defence speech is to listen not only to a great Christian, but also to a clear and logical mind at work. Yet Festus could dismiss him with contemptuous words: 'You are out of your mind, Paul! . . . Your great learning is driving you insane' (Acts 26:24). If one man's spiritual blindness could lead him to dismiss a lucid and rational statement as the raving of a lunatic, it is not surprising if scorn and indifference could lead people in a much more bewildering situation to fling out an accusation of drunkenness. They were facing a phenomenon that they found both baffling and unacceptable. It is not surprising, therefore, if they reacted in a facile way with the only explanation that they could muster.

To turn to Corinth, we ask the two questions: were the tongues heard in worship languages or some kind of ecstatic speech, and were they the same phenomena as appeared on the day of Pentecost? By way of reply there is one general observation to be made. The two authors of the books being considered were not strangers to each other. On the contrary, they were colleagues. It is notable in the narrative of Acts that Troas in chapter 16 marks the beginning of the so-called 'we passages'. Clearly Luke had joined the two missionaries, Paul and Silas. He was to be involved with Paul for the rest of his ministry. He is with Paul when he writes to the Colossians (4:14) and to Philemon (verse 24). He is still with him years later in his final imprisonment (2 Tim 4:11).

It is quite inconceivable that two such close colleagues would not often have discussed together the great events in which they had shared. It is equally inconceivable that they would have made their particular contributions to the growing body of New Testament writings without talking together about the matters on which they were writing. Paul must have known the story of Pentecost. It would surely have been productive of confusion for Paul to use precisely the same terminology as his friend and fellow worker but to mean something different. 'A tongue' in Luke's account meant 'a language', 'a dialect'. If Paul had used the same word and meant by it 'ecstatic speech' it would have been an irresponsible use of words. If an author uses a word that is normally used in a different sense, then his own special usage needs to be spelled out clearly or his readers will be confused. Paul, I suggest, did not need to make any such distinction for the simple reason that 'tongue' meant the same in his letter to Corinth as it did in his friend Luke's account in the book of Acts.

It is important, however, to notice the very different situations. In Acts 2 Luke is describing an unusual occasion. It was festival time and the city would be crowded with pilgrims from far afield. There was thus a situation of linguistic diversity. As far as foreign tongues were concerned, there was an unusual variety of foreign-speaking Jews present for whom such tongues made sense. In Corinth, by contrast, Paul is describing the situation of a local church where, apart from visitors, the bulk of a congregation speaks the same language. If a foreign tongue was spoken in such a context then, unless an interpreter was present, no one would understand. It would sound absolute gibberish.

The average English-speaking person in the United Kingdom tends to speak only English. Indeed his rather dismissive reference to foreigners 'jabbering away' indicates not only his own insular outlook, but also his relegation of other languages to the nonsense area. Of course, often he is rebuked for his nationalistic pride as he admits that the foreigners' words are not really nonsense; it is simply that they sound like that to him. It was precisely like this in Corinth. Greek pride was dismissive of other cultures. Indeed, the very term 'barbarian', which Greeks shared with the Latin-speakers of Rome, showed how they viewed foreigners. To hear tongues in a worship service without an interpreter would sound like the incoherence of a lunatic. This, indeed, is how Paul describes the reaction of the amazed outsiders: 'Will they not say that you are out of your mind?' (1 Cor 14:23).

Turning in closer detail to Paul's words in 1 Corinthians 14, the conclusion seems inescapable that he is employing the word 'tongue' in the sense of 'language'. Thus, in verse 10 he refers to the variety of tongues in the world, all of them with meaning; it is clear that 'tongues' here means 'languages'. Similarly, in verse 21 he refers to men of foreign tongues and again it is clear that 'tongues' means 'languages'. This is all the more evident since he is quoting from the Old Testament where the prophet warns of the foreign invaders whose tongue will be alien to the Jew.

What, then, do we say to the argument that the language is that of heaven? Those who maintain this would quote the first verse of 1 Corinthians 13. Thus, James Dunn argues that '"tongues of men" will denote not simply ordinary human speech but inspired speech of different kinds in the vernacular, while "tongues of angels" will be Paul's and/or the Corinthians' description of *glossolalia*'.[14] The same position is taken by Timothy Pain.[15] Admittedly, he only advances the suggestion as a possibility. However, he goes on to a firmer claim with a quite extraordinary appeal to non-Christian opinion. Ignoring the clear word of Paul that the unregenerate person cannot understand the things that come from the Spirit of God (1 Cor 2:14) he makes the astonishing comment on the tongues used in the fellowship that 'a large enough number of non-Christians has described it as "angelic" to make me take it seriously.'

By way of comment on this suggested understanding of the nature of the tongues at Corinth, we might begin by invoking a rather basic principle as far as interpreting Scripture is concerned. It is always precarious to base any theory on one isolated reference. When that reference is itself debatable as far as interpretation is concerned, the foundation is even more uncertain. An allied principle of interpretation is that it is always wise to argue from the plain passages of Scripture to elucidate the obscure, rather than vice versa. In this case it is a risky procedure to move from this isolated reference to 'angels' when there is detailed and plain evidence elsewhere. It is surely better to base teaching on references that agree with the general picture, rather than fasten on to this one isolated detail.

One must also point out that if, in fact, the tongues of Corinth were the language of the angels, then they would not be the same as the tongues on the day of Pentecost. On that occasion they were quite evidently the languages of men, and Luke is explicit in so describing them. Already in this chapter I have argued that Luke and Paul are using the word 'tongue' in the same sense so that I do not need to repeat the argument.

What needs, however, to be noted in 1 Corinthians 13 is the context. Paul is emphasizing in the most vigorous fashion the utter uselessness of any spiritual activity if it is not accompanied by love. Thus, he surveys various manifestations of deep devotion or sacrificial zeal, and dismisses them all if love is not present. The simplest way of taking the opening verse is to see it, as indeed it is presented, as a hypothetical possibility. Alford interpreted the phrase as 'a case which never has been exemplified.'[16] Paul surveys every conceivable possibility of articulate speech, whether the languages of men, which will feature prominently in his teaching in 1 Corinthians 14, or the language of heaven itself. Were all these possibilities to be realized they would still be futile without love. In short, one may say that whatever the language of the angels may be—the Jewish rabbis used to debate this—Paul is not here discussing tongues but love. The reference to tongues is simply one part of his argument. It is unwise to use an illustration employed in an argument to try and develop a theory!

Many readers may feel that it is so evident that the tongues in the book of Acts and Corinthians are the same phenomenon and are human languages that it is labouring the point to prove this. I sympathize! However, since arguments have been mustered to assert that they are different, it has been necessary to risk boring some readers in order to rebut the notion.

There is another aspect of the gift of a tongue that is common to both narratives and is important to note. In every case it is bestowed by the sovereign God who gives gifts to whom he will and when he will. Luke stresses this point again and again. The account in Acts 2:2 ff. speaks of a sudden happening—the gift was given. The tongues were not induced by some psychological conditioning of the disciples. The wind of God blew straight from heaven. It is the same in Acts 10:44–45: 'The Holy Spirit came on all who heard the message' and the gift was 'poured out even on the Gentiles.' In Acts 19:6 the Holy Spirit is described as exercising the same sovereign ministry: he 'came on them, and they spoke in tongues and prophesied.'

Paul has the same strong emphasis. In 1 Corinthians 12:7 he writes that 'The manifestation of the Spirit is given for the common good.' There is a brief passage detailing some of the gifts. He stresses that each gift is given—it is a sovereign gift from God (1 Cor 12:8, 11). He returns to the same emphasis at the end of the chapter, that behind the variety of gifts is the sovereign giver: 'God has appointed . . . those speaking in different kinds of tongues' (verse 28).

Paul recognizes that the gift has been misused in Corinth. However, he does not go to the extreme of either forbidding the use of tongues in the service of worship or even rejecting the gift completely. He gladly bears testimony to his own experience: 'I thank God that I speak in tongues more than all of you' (1 Cor 14:18). He is strongly emphasizing the surpassing importance of prophecy but he is careful not to denigrate the gift of tongues. He wants to avoid its abuse or over-emphasis. Yet, at the same time he will not let them despise the gift. So while he would prefer them to prophesy, he is none the less quite clear: 'I would like every one of you to speak in tongues' (verse 5). Because of his insistence on a sparing and correct use in public of the gift, he still wants to avoid misunderstanding. The Corinthian believers must not conclude that he wants to banish the gift from congregational life. So he ends the long statement on the subject by a firm rebuke to any who may misconstrue his meaning: 'Do not forbid speaking in tongues' (verse 39).

To appreciate the rules that he lays down for a right use of the gift in public worship, it is important to see what Paul's underlying principles are. There is first of all the principle that governs all the gifts—they are to be used in such a way that they will help to build up the believers spiritually. In the area of public worship this leads to the other principle, namely, that of intelligibility. When Christians come together to worship God, everything that is said or sung must be intelligible, otherwise, how can there be a true participation? So Paul asks the question of those who would be ready to speak in a tongue without any interpretation being provided: 'How can one who finds himself among those who do not understand say "Amen" to your thanksgiving, since he does not know what you are saying?' (1 Cor 14:16).

This implies that the speaker is not so overwhelmed by such a visitation of the Spirit that he cannot control the flow of words from his lips. On the contrary, Paul insists that if there is no translator to interpret, the speaker should be quiet. This does not mean that the one who wants to use his gift should ignore or stifle the urge. It is simply that he must not utter the tongue openly, but he may still 'Speak to himself and God' (1 Cor 14:28).

A vitally important distinction, but one that is sadly often forgotten, lies behind all that Paul says. Distinguishing between tongues and prophecy, he emphasizes that 'Anyone who speaks in a tongue does not speak to men but to God', while in contrast, 'Everyone who prophesies speaks to men' (1 Cor 14:2–3). This important distinction is reinforced by verse 28 where the speaker, although silent publicly, 'Speaks to . . . God.' This has a vital significance in the matter of interpretation. If the content of a message spoken in a tongue is translated into the known language of the congregation, then it must, of necessity, appear as an utterance directed not to men but to God.

When we speak to God we adore and worship, we praise and magnify him, we bring our needs to him, we express our trust in him and our love for him. Obviously we neither command God nor exhort him. He is subject neither to human complaint nor human rebuke. If, then, what purports to be an interpretation of a tongue comes in terms of exhortation or encouragement or command or rebuke—all directed to the congregation—it must surely be ruled out as spurious. It is certainly true that a congregation will be blessed if someone prays or praises. The adoration directed towards God can come as a rebuke, a pressure on us to obey or an encouragement. But it does so indirectly. It is still essentially and primarily addressed to God. So, too, if the words spoken in a tongue are authentic, and if the interpretation is genuine, then the utterance will be heard for what it truly should be, words addressed to God.

In reply to this, it will not do to claim that interpretation may adapt or modify or develop the original message. An interpreter at the United Nations is not a commentator but a translator. His aim must be to render into the language of those to whom he interprets, the foreign language of the speaker, but to keep as closely as he possibly can to the original. It is quite true that one cannot, as an interpreter, translate in a wooden and literal way, since the idioms of one language may not correspond with those in another. Nevertheless, with this proviso, it is still true that the closer the translated words are to the original the more faithful is the interpreter to the task. It is most important that we should recognize that the interpreting of 1 Corinthians 14 should be seen for what it is. It is not a commentary. It is not an exposition. It is the rendering into the known language of the hearers an utterance that came in a tongue foreign to theirs.

It may be claimed that this fails to do justice to the fact that ultimately it is the Holy Spirit who is the interpreter. Surely, it may be argued, he has the sovereign right to develop the utterance he himself prompted. The answer to this is the basic premise of this book, that he is the Spirit of truth. He cannot, therefore, contradict himself. It was the Spirit himself who moved Paul to write that 'Anyone who speaks in a tongue does not speak to men but to God' (1 Cor 14:2). It would be a denial of his essential character for him to go completely contrary to what he has said and to move someone to give an interpretation that violates this basic assertion. The Holy Spirit is not, however, the author of such confusion. If he prompts someone to speak in a tongue directed to God, then he will prompt the interpreter to give to the congregation an utterance in their own mother tongue which is also directed to God.

This principle of intelligibility has application to any united use of tongues such as singing together. This practice is widespread, but one must ask, is it consistent with the revelation that the Spirit of truth has given us in the Scriptures? The answer must surely be that it is not. One leader admitted in personal conversation that he had to acknowledge that they did not have strong scriptural warrant for the practice. My reply was that it was not a case of having inadequate scriptural support for the practice, but rather a fact that there was strong scriptural warrant against it.

How can anyone say the 'Amen'? Paul's question presses in insistently. His further firm contention must be noted, that if an outsider comes into the assembly he will think they are mad. For Paul, writing under the Spirit's direction, this would be a justified charge, yet one for which he believes no occasion should be given. If such an outsider came in and there was intelligible prophecy, then by God's grace he could be enlightened and led to Christ.

Paul reinforces the argument by appealing to the Old Testament prophecy. Isaiah warned a disobedient people that the foreign tongues of an invading army would be the sign of God's judgement upon them. The foreign tongue would not encourage or enthuse them. It would, rather, tell them by its unintelligible words that the aliens were entering destructively into the temple of God. So says Paul, as he applies the prophecy, tongues without interpretation are a judgement sign to unbelievers. They will neither encourage them to seek nor enlighten them. Rather, such unintelligible utterances will lead to their total dismissal of the gospel and so to their perdition.

It is for this reason that Paul at this point is so explicit. Here are specific regulations to keep things under a godly control. There must be no more than two who speak in a tongue—or at most three. The very fact that he puts it in this way indicates that he sees three such speakers as being the ultimate limit. Even these two or three must not speak openly unless there is an interpreter. This last-named requirement is not an optional extra. Paul spells it out as definitely as could possibly be done: 'Someone must interpret' (1 Cor 14:27). Indeed, if someone is so stupid or misguided as to misunderstand this very plain statement he reinforces it by adding: 'If there is no interpreter, the speaker should keep quiet in the church and speak to himself and God' (verse 28).

It will not do to try and counter these firm directions by putting 'singing in a tongue' in a different category from 'speaking in a tongue'. Paul has already ruled out that possibility. Earlier in his argument he puts the two forms of utterance in the same category: 'I will pray with my spirit, but I will also pray with my mind; I will sing with my spirit, but I will also sing with my mind' (1 Cor 14:15).

Both of these statements are in the context of his firm insistence on everything publicly uttered being understandable to all the people.

It is very hard to see how Paul's words could ever be used to justify any kind of speaking in a tongue or singing in a tongue in unison. He is again so explicit in his statement. Having limited such speakers to two or at most three, he lays down precisely that they must do so 'One at a time' (1 Cor 14:27). It is perhaps significant that he adds that one and one only was to interpret. There is no question of interpreters 'one at a time' for that could have meant profitless discussion. The English translation here, 'someone must interpret', is misleading, since Paul uses the Greek numeral 'one' to emphasize one only. This, however, reinforces the contention that far from permitting even two to speak in tongues at the same time, they must do so 'one at a time' and one interpreter could then deal with one message.

Paul clearly envisages the possibility that there may be no one present able to interpret: 'If there is no interpreter, the speaker should keep quiet' (1 Cor 14:28). This suggests that the speaker himself might not be able to interpret the words. It also suggests that the gift of tongue-speaking was much more frequent than the ability to interpret. This again points towards the fact that the gift of speaking in a tongue is designed much more for private rather than congregational use.

He stresses this point further as he underlines the need to instruct others. He is in no way depreciating the value of tongues. How could he, since he has declared that they are a gift of the Holy Spirit. Indeed, he himself uses this gift extensively. Yet he adds the emphatic reminder that public use is a different matter: 'In the church I would rather speak five intelligible words to instruct others than ten thousand words in a tongue' (1 Cor 14:19).

One further question must be faced. Is the gift of

tongues the essential sign of being filled with the Spirit, or as others would describe it, 'being baptized in the Spirit'? If the answer to that question were to be 'yes', then clearly any Christian who has not received this particular charisma might well feel that he or she had not really made the grade spiritually. Indeed, it has been one of the contributory factors in some of our present sad divisions that some have understandably reacted to their dismissal by some of their elitist brethren as virtually second-class citizens in the kingdom. Of course, not all who teach that speaking in a tongue is the test of being filled with the Spirit are guilty of such sinful elitism. Yet it is implicit in their contention, even if they avoid the explicit and hurtful statement. The more important issue, however, is whether the Scripture supports their position. I contend that it does not.

To insist on the essential character of this gift is to run completely contrary to Paul's whole argument in 1 Corinthians 12. There are two basic principles in this argument. The first one is that the Spirit is sovereign in giving his gifts. The second is that the church as the body of Christ has diversity within its basic unity. The conclusions to which Paul points as he expounds these principles is that the variety of gifts within the church is there by virtue of the sovereign disposition of the Spirit, and also because of the varied functions of the different members. So, on the one hand, no one member has all the gifts and, on the other, no one gift is given to all the members.

Paul spells this out in precise detail as he lists some of the charismata. Having laid down his basic principle that 'There are different kinds of gifts, but the same Spirit' (1 Cor 12:4) he then specifies some of these gifts. There is a very clear demarcation between different members of the body in the apportioning of these gifts. Thus, he carefully emphasizes the diversity of gifts given 'To one ... to another ... to another ...' etc. He reinforces this emphasis on diversity by the explicit statement: 'All these are the work of one and the same Spirit, and he gives them to each one, just as he determines' (verse 11). Just as the gifts of healings or the gift of prophecy were quite specifically given to some but not to others so equally, appearing as it does in the same list and with the same underlying principles involved, the gift of tongues is given to some and not to others.

Paul confirms this conclusion by his subsequent argument. He contends that just as in a body every limb is important and has its own function, so it is in the body of Christ. Each believer has a unique role and is equipped by the Spirit to fulfil a distinctive ministry. No one Christian has a monopoly of graces or gifts. No single believer has a sufficiency that would enable him to be independent of his fellows. Each one has a distinctive and individual contribution to the life of the body. To contribute thus requires the special endowment by the Holy Spirit.

Paul continues the same emphasis as he summarizes his argument. Having underlined the basics once again: 'Now you are the body of Christ, and each one of you is a part of it' (1 Cor 12:27), he enumerates God's appointed ministries within the church. It is very much like a classified list with 'First . . . second . . . third . . . then . . . also . . .' There could not be a sharper differentiation of gifts, and one of these is the gift of tongues. If any doubt were left, it would surely be dismissed by his final series of rhetorical questions. In each case the obvious answer is 'No'. Yet one of these questions is precisely the one with which this particular discussion started: 'Do all speak in tongues?' (verse 30). The answer is the same as to the other questions: 'No!'

An attempt has been made to evade what seems to be so plain by conceding that Paul clearly denies that all speak in tongues, yet qualifying this concession by claiming that he is referring to public ministry in a tongue. The answer to this argument is simply to point out that Paul in chapter 12 is not dealing with the control of the gifts in public worship. His argument is, rather, based on the distinct yet complementary functioning of limbs in a body, which is the analogy for the mutually supportive gifts within the body of Christ. It is only in chapter 14 that he turns to the regulating of tongues in the public worship of the church. To read that into the references in chapter 12 is simply to import a qualification that is not present in Paul's actual words.

There has been one unhappy development drawn from the opposite contention that this gift is essential for all. It is the practice of trying to induce it. So the advice is given to leave the tongue limp, as it were, and to avoid speaking one's own mother tongue. There may even be the suggestion of trying to make some sounds. This may achieve results, but they will be the outcome of psychological manifestation or suggestion. It is all so remote from what happened in Acts 2 and in Corinth. There the tongues were not induced, but given by the sovereign bestowal of the Spirit.

The conclusion that seems clear from the whole discussion is that Paul sees the use of the gift as primarily for personal and private use. The fact that he uses the gift so much himself and wants them all to enjoy the same gift (1 Cor 14:5, 18) is matched by the firm restrictions on public utterance. At an early stage in his argument he made the point that the Christian who speaks in a tongue edifies himself (verse 4). This is in no way an incentive to selfishness. It is simply a statement of fact. Furthermore, the restriction on public utterance will not mean that the one who wants to speak openly in a tongue will be spiritually impoverished at that point: 'Let him speak to himself and to God' (1 Cor 14:27) and he will edify himself.

Public worship is a very different matter from a personal time of communion with God. The constant New Testament emphasis is on fellowship, which means sharing and involvement. Anything that hinders such sharing must be ruled out. Every aspect of the service, every word spoken or sung—all must be available to the minds of the worshippers. Intelligibility is the prerequisite to true response. It is as men and women enlightened by the Spirit are able to hear and understand that they are also able to say the 'Amen'. Prophecy, interpreted tongues, psalms, hymns and spiritual songs in the mother tongue of the congregation—all of these will edify and instruct. It is from the standpoint of intelligent participation that believers will be able to offer the sacrifice of praise and thanksgiving.

14

Let Love Have the Last Word!

No one could ever accuse Paul of belittling the exercise of the gifts of the Spirit within the life of the church. Nor could he possibly be construed as merely tolerating their presence without much enthusiasm. He has made it clear in 1 Corinthians 12 that he sees the gifts as a gracious resource granted by the Spirit to enable Christians to function within the Christian fellowship in such a way that they will strengthen, encourage and bless each other. Implicit in all that he has said, and in what he will say in chapter 14, is his concern for a loving relationship to be the major characteristic of the church. The very phrase that is central to his aim is that the gifts are 'for the common good'. This implies the centrality of love.

However, he has seen too much evidence of the misuse of the gifts to imagine mistakenly that the possession of the charismata guarantees either holiness or harmony within the church. He is too aware of the strength and persistence of indwelling sin in the Christian, and the sublety of Satan who uses both the old nature of the believer and the appeal of the standards of the world in order to corrupt the life of the church. Indeed, because of our sinfulness, the very gifts that God gives for our profit can be so misused that they become a hindrance rather than a help.

This in no way implies that there is something defective in the gifts. The fault, rather, is in those who employ them in the wrong way. It is like the small boy who uses his brand new football to cause deliberate hurt to another boy by excluding him from the game in which others have been asked to join. It is like the girl whose new dress has been lovingly provided by her parents but who misuses her present to crow over her neighbour, towards whom she harbours a secret grudge. By contrast, a child may get additional pleasure from the birthday gift because it can be shared with others and all of them benefit.

In Corinth they had been behaving like selfish children. God had been especially gracious to them and had endowed them to a marked degree with spiritual gifts. However, instead of humble gratitude, which would have been appropriate, they had displayed an elitism, as if they themselves were the source of what was only too evidently a gift. Instead of asking themselves how they could most usefully employ their gifts for the benefit of the church, they were so dominated by self-centred excitement that their own ambitions and the display of their gifts to win the hoped-for admiration of others were their major reactions. Instead of a harmony enhanced by the contribution of gifted people, there was a sorry discord.

Paul, however, did not react by rejecting the gifts. That for him would have been rejecting the ministry of the Spirit. It would have been a breach of the kind of word he gave to the Thessalonians: 'Do not put out the Spirit's fire (1 Thess 5:19). That, sadly, is the over-reaction all too common today. The objectors see evidence—and unhappily they don't need to look too far to find it—that charismatic experience can be followed by proud superiority, dismissive attitudes to other Christians and divided churches. They then blame the gifts rather than those who misuse them. It is like blaming the parents for giving the dress to their daughter and then putting the dress in the dustbin! A much better way would be to deal with the girl and, if need be, punish her, and so teach her how to use her present in the right way.

Paul does not react in the wrong way. He continues to recognize that the Spirit is the source of the charismata. He continues to value the gifts for the blessing God may bring to the church through them. He neither implies a censure on the giver, nor foolishly denigrates and rejects the gifts. Rather, he fastens the blame firmly where it belongs, and shows Christians a better way. He not only exposes their sinful misuse of the gifts and rebukes them for this, but turns them to the great principle that should govern their lives in general, and their use of the charismata in particular. Love stands supreme and love must be the dominating influence in life, in worship and in witness.

It is Paul's indignation that God's gifts should be misused that leads him to speak with such passion. Do they think that the mere possession of a charisma enhances the status of the Christian? Do they imagine that a self-opinionated display, or an unconcerned attitude are really incidental? Are they so excited by the evidence of supernatural power among them that they do not see the ultimate goal of God's powerful working? Well, let them realize that the possession of a gift without the exercise of love is just nothing at all. Far from preening themselves on their spiritual wealth, they should be thoroughly ashamed that they have so grievously squandered that wealth on themselves. Their proud boast that they belonged to a richly charismatic church falls on deaf ears as far as Paul is concerned. All he sees is the conceit, the self-interest, the utter lack of concern for others. Away with all their pretensions. They are really spiritual nonentities—they are 'Nothing' (1 Cor 13:2).

It is significant that Paul writes in the first person. He knew his own heart. He knew only too well the spiritual perils of his own situation. He surely had himself in mind, as well as his readers, when he wrote earlier in the letter: 'So, if you think you are standing firm, be careful that you don't fall!' (1 Cor 10:12). He knew that he had to keep the firm hand of discipline on himself, 'So that after I have preached to others, I myself will not be disqualified for the prize' (1 Cor 9:27). So he includes himself and, by implication, every Christian in this warning passage. A Christian may be a superb preacher or may have the gift of speaking in another tongue, but in either case, without love the words that flow so easily are in the ears of God a clashing discord.

The same applies to that cardinal gift, the faith that can achieve the impossible. If love is not governing its exercise, then it is so worthless that the one who possesses it is dismissed as being of no value at all. Even if the service being rendered for God and the church leads to great personal sacrifice, and even martyrdom, it is utterly pointless. Without love the greatest attainments, the highest achievements, the most passionate zeal—all are cancelled and rejected as worthless.

What is this love? It is certainly not the reaction to others that the world has in mind when it uses the word. 'Love' in current usage is simply lust embellished with a fine title. It is like a woman modestly dressed who turns out to be a prostitute. It is that kind of 'love' that is so lightly declared, so glibly offered and that is as easily withdrawn and transferred to some other person.

Nor is this love the general friendly benevolence one meets in many people who are not Christians. The common grace of God often produces in sinful men and women attitudes of marked concern for others' needs. Then also there are those whose temperament, coupled with a background of security, produces a genial and caring attitude. I am reminded of Dr Lloyd-Jones' comment, 'There are nice dogs and nasty dogs, but they are still dogs. And there are nice sinners and nasty sinners, but they are still sinners.' The love of which Paul writes is neither lustful desire nor general kindly benevolence.

This love is so special that in the language of the New Testament a distinctive word is used—*agape*. Its standard is nothing less than the love of God. 'God is love' (1 Jn 4:16). It belongs to the very essence of his being. Implicit in this statement that God is love is the fact that the love of God is prior to creation. This prompts the question: how was love possible when there were no possible objects of that love, men and women not yet having been created? The answer to that is the biblical doctrine of the Trinity. God is not a solitary unity with no possibility of expressing his life and love. God is One, but within that unity of being there are three persons, the Father, the Son and the Holy Spirit. Thus, prior to creation, within the rich life of God there was an inter-personal relationship that made love both possible and actual. God's love for men and women is thus the echo of the love of each person within the Trinity. It is not a divine activity that developed when humanity first appeared. It is fundamental to the very being of God. It is eternal.

Because this is so, all his actions are the outflow of this love. That is why God's love is displayed so freely. He does not show favour to those from whom he has benefited. He does not love those who he hopes will love him in response. Were this to be the situation no human being would ever be the recipient of his love. What makes God's love so remarkable is that it is extended to those who have no love for him and, indeed, may reject him and hate him. This was to Paul the supreme wonder of the cross of Christ. 'God demonstrates his own love for us in this: While we were still sinners, Christ died for us' (Rom 5:8).

In that same chapter in the letter to the Romans, Paul

sees the emergence of that love in the life of men and women as being one element in the work of God when he brings a sinner to Christ. When we trust God's promises and believe on the Lord Jesus we are freely forgiven. We are accepted as righteous and granted a free access to God. We begin to taste the joy of God, and this gives a new assurance for the future and a glad readiness to face trouble, knowing that God's love will use such trials for our blessing. What enables us to face life with a new attitude is the gift of the Holy Spirit through whose coming to us 'God has poured out his love into our hearts' (Rom 5:5).

If, then, the miracle of the new birth means the sharing of the life of God, then it means also participation in that distinctive love of God. This leads to the further conclusion that if God's love has been displayed in his readiness to give his Son for us, and if Christ's love has been seen in his sacrifice of himself for us, then this new love that has been born in our hearts will lead us in the direction of self-denial and self-sacrifice. Loving God involves a radical reorientation of our lives as we are turned from the inward-looking concerns of the sinner to the new aim of living to the glory of God. Since this love in us is God's life showing its presence in our hearts, it should also redirect our selfish thinking to a new goal, which is the well being of others.

The emergence of this love in our hearts is affected by the power of the Holy Spirit. It is the same Spirit who will direct and deepen that love until its final glory in heaven, when perfect love shall sweep us into the joy of the worship around the throne. The Spirit, however, is not to be thought of in impersonal terms, as if he were a permanent channel of God's love to us. He is revealed in Scripture as a person. He may be disobeyed. He may be grieved. He may withdraw his gracious operation from us. If, then, this love of his is to flow steadily into our lives, and through our lives to others, we must live in obedient submission to the Spirit's directions.

There is, therefore, no conflict between an emphasis on the fruit of the Spirit and the gifts of the Spirit. If one side is stressed and the other neglected, there is a very serious imbalance that can have spiritually-damaging results. The biblical balance requires that both are kept in view. The fruit of the Spirit is the maturing development of character in which he leads the Christian to mortify indwelling sin, to cultivate the graces of the gospel and to aim at a holiness that reflects the perfect holiness of God. The gifts of the Spirit, on the other hand, are the abilities that the Spirit imparts to enable us to serve one another. To over-emphasize holiness at the expense of service or to over-emphasize gifts at the expense of love are both wrong. It is when Christians are aiming at a holy life, and at the same time utilizing their spiritual gifts in loving care for others, that the fellowship of the Holy Spirit is realized in a local congregation.

Paul's great chapter on love is not only a necessary corrective to excesses and false attitudes, but also, positively, it emphasizes the point that any discussion of charismatic issues should have a pastoral motive. Paul is not engaged in a theological discussion of the gifts of the Spirit in some academic way. Nor should our debates be conducted, as unhapppily they often are, as if it was a theoretical argument. His concern was, and ours must also be, that God's people should so grasp the significance of the Spirit's gifts that they will be better equipped to minister one to another within the body of Christ.

As Paul spells out in some detail the outworking of love, we see not only a pattern of conduct but a reflection of the life of Jesus who perfectly embodied in human experience the love of God. As we read the words 'Love is patient', we hear an echo of Peter's words: 'When they hurled their insults at him, he did not retaliate; when he suffered, he made no threats' (1 Pet 2:23). So, patient love is ready to face provocation without hitting back. That provocation may come because of another's tactlessness and insensitive attitude. It can be the product of someone's ingratitude, especially when the opposite might have been expected. Shakespeare in King Lear underlined that ingratitude in the famous words: 'How sharper than a serpent's tooth it is to have a thankless child.' Provocation may come finally from the deliberate intention of another to hurt. Unkind actions, harsh wards, petty persecution—how provoking they can be.

Love, however, does not respond with the normal human reaction. When people are hurt they can reply with impatience, with annoyed irritation, or with blazing indignation. They will even boast with some pride that they can give as good as they get! If they are in a subordinate position they may have to endure in silence, but it is not the calm of patient endurance. Rather, it is the lid firmly clamped on the seething pot, which overflows in bitter words when the offender is no longer present. In the face of all this, love learns to look to God for strength to control the reaction. Love recalls the patience of God himself when faced with extreme provocation. Love stirs the memory of those who feel so deeply hurt to recall how far more deeply they themselves have hurt God.

So love checks the bitter thoughts that clamour for ugly expression in vitriolic words. Love recognizes the hardening attitude from which unspoken words of anger are beginning to form. Love hears another voice: 'Father, forgive them, for they do not know what they are doing' (Lk 23:34). It was a prayer echoed by Stephen as he was brutally and unjustly stoned to death: 'Lord, do not hold this sin against them' (Acts 7:60). Love learns that there is a better way than angry retaliation. It is the way of forgiving of which Paul writes to the Ephesians: 'Do not grieve the Holy Spirit of God, with whom you were sealed for the day of redemption. Get rid of all bitterness, rage and anger, brawling and slander, along with every form of malice. Be kind and compassionate to one another, forgiving each other, just as in Christ God forgave you' (Eph 4:30–32).

Such love is not only patient in the face of provocation, it is also kind in its concern for others. Love in its kindness feels for those in need and does not restrict its help to those who fall within the category of friends or of congenial and responsive people. Like the love of the good Samaritan, it enlarges its horizons of compassion, and stretches across man-made barriers. It does not wait for a sense of duty to thrust the needs of others into its line of vision. Rather, love is on the alert for opportunities to show the kindness of a caring God who 'causes his sun to rise on the evil and the good, and sends rain on the righteous and the unrighteous' (Mt 5:45). This word of Jesus was by way of reinforcing his command in the previous verse: 'Love your enemies and pray for those who persecute you'. It is love in action!

Love is not only positively active, it also has a negative aspect in that it aims to avoid attitudes, words and deeds that would conflict with love's aim to benefit others. Paul continues about love: 'It is not self-seeking'. This, of course, does not mean the rejection of legitimate aims and ambitions. After all, the Scriptures are very insistent that diligence should be a characteristic of the believer: 'Go to the ant, you sluggard; consider its ways and be wise!' (Prov 6:6) and 'Whatever your hand finds to do, do it with all your might' (Eccles 9:10). If God has given us skills of hand or brain, if he has endowed us with gifts of various kinds, then it should be our aim to glorify our Creator by stretching ourselves to the limit, aiming at realizing the full potential that God has granted us.

What Paul is really rejecting here is the self-love that is so determined to realize selfish ambition that it is prepared to cut the corners of ethical principle, and is ready to turn a blind eye to the needs of others, or even to trample on them in the scramble to reach a personal goal. Self-love, the sorry evidence of original sin, shows itself at an early age in the petulant demands of a child and in his or her sulky moods when thwarted. It is seen in the young person who cheats at games or 'cogs' in examinations. It corrupts sport, politics and social life. It ultimately reaches its more ugly manifestation in family quarrels, broken homes and, finally, in the supremely selfish display of war.

The world acclaims those who reach the top by whatever means. The title 'Great' has been given to the conquering generals like Alexander of Macedon and Charles of the Holy Roman Empire. Those who are admired today are the dominant figures in human activity, even if their rise to pre-eminence has been ruthless. Tragically, that same mentality can enter the church of God. John writes of 'Diotrephes, who loves to be first' (3 Jn 9). In Corinth it was this corrupting desire to excel that had led to such misuse of the gifts of the Spirit. It leads to a similar misuse today!

Love, by contrast, 'Does not envy, it does not boast, it is not proud. It is not rude, it is not self-seeking, it is not easily angered, it keeps no record of wrongs' (1 Cor 13:4–5). Here is a cumulative description of a life in which a firm 'No' is said to self. The desire to display one's gifts or to draw attention to one's achievements is seen for what it is, a symptom of the sinful pride that needs to be trodden underfoot. Love does not excuse but condemns the tendency to be quickly angered by others. It is not touchy. It does not brood sullenly on old resentments. It does not carry a permanent chip on the shoulder. Having seen the hollow emptiness of self-seeking, love lifts its eyes to see more wonderful goals. The glory of God, the blessing of fellow Christians, the salvation of the lost— these are the goals that love pursues with keen endeavour.

Paul enters a necessary corrective lest anyone should think that love is so gentle that it can condone evil, or so embracing that it will tolerate false teaching. Love is not sentimental, nor is it soft and flabby. The loving Jesus could still indignantly chase the money-changers from the temple, and rebuke in biting words the Pharisees as they led men astray. Love sees not just the evil doer or the false prophet, but sees beyond to the physical harm, the moral damage and the spiritual havoc that they cause. So love has room for indignation. It has no place for the anger that springs from personal hurt, but it certainly endorses the passion that resists the evil that destroys others, and exposes and rejects the heresies that lead others astray.

Love, by contrast, is a close friend of the truth. Here is the rebuttal of the thinking that puts sound doctrine and spiritual experience into two separate and almost opposing camps. So the caricatures are paraded. There is the preacher who is cast in the role of the dour, ponderous and dull advocate of rather stodgy doctrine. At the other extreme are the wild zealots who are feverishly looking for fresh excitement, and retailing claims of marvellous happenings. As often in caricature, there are gleams of truth, for sadly there are those at either extreme who sometimes seem to justify the descriptions. They are, however, still caricatures, for love and truth are not opposed. They are boon companions, and so close is their friendship that, like any close relationship, it is accompanied by joy.

So the believer rejoices in the truth, delighting in the whole counsel of God, revelling in the great doctrines of God's grace, and speaking with exhilaration of the gospel. When a preacher has such love in his heart, he does not simply churn out his well-prepared and cogently-argued discourses. He preaches with fire in his bones and with a passionate delight in the doctrines he preaches. Because love rejoices in the truth, it cannot remain content to speak only of the truth in the careful and measured formulations of doctrinal statements. It certainly does want such statements to guide it along right paths, but love's joy in the truth goes further, and spills over in glad testimony. It finds further expression, as love often does, in poetry. It wants to match that poetry with music. So love's delight in the truth prompts the Christian to sing with exuberance and exaltation of spirit. That is why the great hymns and songs of the church have a blend of biblical doctrine and personal response.

Paul recognized this joy that love has in the truth when he wrote to the Ephesians. He had doubtless heard drunkards singing their bawdy songs and getting some temporary pleasure from their music. That, however, is not for the Christian. So he warns: 'Do not get drunk on wine, which leads to debauchery. Instead, be filled with the Spirit' (Eph 5:18). How, then, will this fullness be shown? Well, since the Spirit shed abroad God's love in our hearts, it will be seen in the deepening of our love. But since this love rejoices in the truth, it will manifest itself further. Not only will there be a grateful response to God for the truth that he has revealed in Scripture, but there will also be a desire to share those doctrines with others. That will be done in the preaching and teaching that are the hallmarks of a true church. It will also be achieved as, in a loving fellowship, Christians share in joyful song and at the same time share in the truths of Scripture.

So Paul follows his call to be filled with the Spirit with the further summons: 'Speak to one another with psalms, hymns and spiritual songs. Sing and make music in your heart to the Lord' (Eph 5:19). In a parallel passage in Colossians, he indicates the content of such song. It is not sentimentality dressed up in rhyme. Rather, it is doctrine set to music, and again it is in the context of a loving congregation: 'Let the peace of Christ rule in your hearts, since as members of one body you were called to peace. And be thankful. Let the word of Christ dwell in you richly as you teach and admonish one another with all wisdom, and as you sing psalms, hymns and spiritual songs with gratitude in your hearts to God' (Col 3:15–16). Here are some of the marks of a congregation where love rejoices in the truth. The preaching is on fire. The fellowship is characterized by mutual concern. Sheer delight in the truth overflows in glad songs of praise to God.

Love is gentle in dealing with failure in others. The Revised Version recognized the problem of translating the first of the four verbs used in 1 Corinthians 13:7. So it translates it as did the Authorized Version, 'Love beareth all things'. In the margin, however, the revisers put the alternative meaning of the Greek verb: 'covereth'. Judging by the context, the latter meaning seems to be better. The word is used in Greek in the sense of throwing a veil of silence over someone. It is surely in this sense that Paul uses it here as he goes on to speak of believing the best about people and hoping the best from them.

The malice of the world delights to expose the failures and wrongdoings of others. That is why there is such a relish in the press descriptions of the sordid, the dishonest and the salacious—and that is also why such newspapers have such huge circulations. People have no great interest in stable homes, honest businesses and reliable politicians. They have, however, an intense interest in the moral failures, the shame, the dishonesty and the murky backgrounds that ruthless reporting dredges up for their perverted interest.

It is a sad fact of life that gossip and general tittle-tattle focus on failure rather than success, on shame rather than on glory. Love, by contrast, does not unnecessarily expose the failure. When forced, for the sake of the well being of the church, to expose wrongdoing and to impose discipline, it takes no pleasure in so doing. It prefers to speak personally to the other's conscience and, as far as is possible, to cover the failure with an unspoken understanding which, in God's mercy, may lead the wrongdoer to repentance.

Allied to this refusal to publicize failure is love's readiness to attribute right motives. There is nothing more calculated to discourage someone who has failed and to block the path to repentance than a suspicious attitude that makes a bad situation worse. The old saying about giving a dog a bad name is so true; it tends to prompt the reaction that he might as well earn it! Love, however, does not always suspect false motives. Love does not assume that past failure means a present conspiracy to avoid detection. Love is ready to trust even if sometimes that trust is betrayed.

That does not mean that love is gullible. There are plausible rogues abroad. There are confidence tricksters whose ready flow of words covers over their dishonest ways. There are false prophets who, in Jesus' words, 'Come to you in sheep's clothing, but inwardly they are ferocious wolves' (Mt 7:15). In such cases love indicates exposure rather than concealment. It prompts an alert attitude rather than a credulous acceptance. But with this proviso, we return to the main thrust of Paul's words, which clearly indicate a generous attitude and a readiness to encourage the one who has done wrong.

In this context it is good to remember love's close link with patience. So love hopes on in face of past disappointment. Of course, this does not mean a credulity that takes no account of the past, especially if there is no present evidence of true sorrow for sin. If a man is detected in dishonesty and lying, then it is folly to go blithely forward as if he could be given implicit trust. On the other hand, love does not shrug the shoulders with a dismissive attitude that says, in so many words, 'He's a hopeless case'. How many backsliders have been brought back by the loving concern that looked into a very uncertain future and still hoped on?

Love persists. Instead of the aggrieved attitude or the impatient word or the irritable response, love continues to face discouragement and disappointment. Love is thus able to persist, not only because it can often look back to the love of God shown at Calvary, and to the providential love of God ever since, but because it can look forward to the coming glory. Glory dawns in Emmanuel's land. And what is that coming glory? It is the delight of a shared experience when the pettiness, the quarrels, the misunderstandings, will all be in the past, and where the united worship will be a great song of praise to the God who loved us so much as to give his Son, and to the Christ whose love took him even to the cross.

Love exposes and rebukes the pride that is so persistent even in the life of the believer. Love checks the divisiveness that so often creeps into our fellowships. Love corrects the imbalance of an undue obsession with the gifts of the Spirit that puts us in danger of losing sight of the Giver as well as the needs of those who should benefit through the exercise of our gifts. Love is the greatest gift of all and is the primary fruit.

It is primary even in the company of faith and hope. Faith is of cardinal importance, but faith needs the fire of love to restrain it from becoming a mere intellectual acquaintance with God. Hope is also an essential element. Yet if hope is not supported and enthused by love, it can sink into a dogged endurance. Love lifts the heart of the believer towards God. Love keeps hope alive even in the darkest night, for reunion with the beloved lies ahead. Love needs faith for faith lays hold on the revelation of God in his word. Love needs hope for there must be a future consummation if love is not to wilt and fade. All three are vital, 'But,' says Paul, 'the greatest of these is love' (1 Cor 13:13).

It is a mark of our worldliness that too often we are less excited by the evidence of love in a church than we are by phenomena which, though important as evidence of the working of the Holy Spirit, are none the less passing in their effects. We hear some speak with gratification of their congregation where they enjoy a powerful expository ministry. We hear others who tell with delight of healings that have stirred the people. We can be thankful for powerful preaching, for lively worship and for spiritual gifts being exercised. Yet how often have we heard people becoming excited and talking of the love that has been shed abroad in their fellowship? We may hear outsiders speak of exciting things they have seen or heard, but how often have we heard them speak as the pagans spoke in the early centuries: 'How these Christians love one another!'? Let Paul summarize it: 'Eagerly desire the greater gifts. And now I will show you the most excellent way . . . . Follow the way of love' (1 Corinthians 12:31; 14:1).

Index of Names

Scripture Index

Notes

Chapter 2
1. K. & D. Ranaghan, *Catholic Pentecostals* (Paulist Press, Deus Books, 1969), pp. 30, 68, 70, 178. T. Flyn, *The Charismatic Renewal and the Irish Experience* (Hodder & Stoughton, 1974), p. 171. Cardinal Suenens, *Ecumenism and Charismatic Renewal* (Darton, Longman & Todd, 1978), pp. 78–80. Rene Laurentin, *Catholic Pentecostalism* (Darton, Longman & Todd, 1977), pp. 192ff.

Chapter 3
2. Leonard Verduin, *The Reformers and Their Stepchildren* (Paternoster, 1964), p. 6.
3. Victor Budgen, *The Charismatics and the Word of God* (Evangelical Press, 1985), p. 89.
4. John Owen, *A Discourse on the Holy Spirit* (A. Macauley, 1972), Vol 3, chapter 5, pp. 178–179.

Chapter 4
5. John Stott, *Baptism and Fullness* (Inter-Varsity Press, 1975), p. 29.
6. David Watson, *You Are My God* (Hodder & Stoughton, 1983), p. 55.

Chapter 7
7. D. M. Lloyd-Jones, 'The Supernatural in Medicine' in *Healing and Medicine* (Kingsway Publications, 1987), p. 66.
8. Henry Frost, *Miraculous Healing* (Marshall, Morgan & Scott, 1951), p. 80.

Chapter 10
9. Trench, *Miracles of Our Lord* (George Routledge & Sons), p. 7.
10. Leslie B. Flyn, *Nineteen Gifts of the Spirit* (Victor Books, 1975), p. 143.
11. William Hendriksen, *An Exposition of the Gospel of John* (Banner of Truth Trust, 1982), p. 272.

Chapter 12
12. Wayne Grudem, *The Gift of Prophecy in 1 Corinthians* (Cambridge University Press of America, 1982), pp. 33–43.
13. B. J. Kidd (ed.), *Documents Illustrative of the History of the Church* (SPCK, 1920).

Chapter 13
14. James Dunn, *Jesus and the Spirit* (SCM, 1975), p. 244.
15. Timothy Pain, *Ashburnham Insights: Tongues and Explanations* (Kingsway Publications, 1986), p. 15.
16. Henry Alford, *The Greek New Testament* (Rivinotons, 1868), vol 2, p. 553.

Joy Unspeakable

by D. Martyn Lloyd-Jones

What does it mean to be baptized with the Holy Spirit?

Can I be a Christian and still not baptized with the Spirit?

What difference will the baptism with the Spirit make in my Christian life?

Straightforward, powerful and with disarming candour, Doctor Lloyd-Jones expounds the Scriptures on an issue that has both united and sadly divided Christians everywhere. Drawing on the experiences of great men of God in years gone by, he challenges us to examine the Scriptures without prejudice, and encourages us to seek the Lord for all the blessing and equipping that he is pleased to give.

K Kingsway Publications

Prove All Things
The Sovereign Work of the Holy Spirit

by D. Martyn Lloyd-Jones

Large format paperback

In *Joy Unspeakable*, Dr Lloyd-Jones showed that nothing short of a baptism with the Holy Spirit is needed to endue the church with power and authority in its proclamation of the truth.

In this companion volume he looks at the related question of the gifts of the Spirit and their place in God's purposes. In his usual lucid and compelling manner, he examines the teaching of Scripture concerning the gifts freely given at the sovereign discretion of the Spirit. Conscious of the enemy's activity in this realm, he helps us steer a course between the extremes of undiscerning enthusiasm and a spirit of unbelief. Only then can we move forward with confidence and demonstrate the power of God in a needy world.

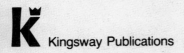 Kingsway Publications

Power Evangelism and The Word of God

by Donald Bridge

Do we need better preaching or more miracles in the church today? *Proclamation* of the gospel, or *manifestations* of the Holy Spirit?

Many Christians champion the virtues of solid preaching as the central task of the church. Others prefer to emphasize signs and wonders as the acid test of God's activity. But few have made any real attempt to marry the two together.

There are tensions. But in this book Donald Bridge gives a heart cry not to miss a golden opportunity to work together as we seek God for revival in our land.

Donald Bridge is known for his ministry of reconciliation, especially through books such as *The Water That Divides* and *The Meal That Unites* (written with David Phypers). In this book he draws on his experiences from several different countries to throw light on one of the most crucial questions facing the church today.

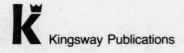
Kingsway Publications

Chosen for Good

by Peter Lewis, Roy Clements and Greg Haslam

Edited by Robert Horn

Large format paperback

Three men, endowed with a remarkable gift of teaching,
expound the basics of the Christian gospel. Here we see
man in his need, in utter degradation and hopelessness.
Yet we also see God in his glory, choosing to bring lost
men and women back into the light of his presence and
showering on them the blessings of eternal life.

In this book we learn—

    — how God sees mankind today
    — what he has decided to do about man's plight
    — the meaning of Christ's death on the cross
    — how we can believe the gospel
    — how we can know God will never let us go

The authors guide us carefully through the theological
minefield that has been laid around these great truths,
and helpfully apply them to our everyday lives. As such
it is ideal not only for new Christians, but for all those
who wish to gain a deeper appreciation of what God has
done for us in Christ.

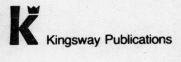

Kingsway Publications